This book doesn't pull any punches . . . . The advice contained in this volume, its logical organization, its developmentally appropriate sequencing, and its lack of "other party bashing," makes it "must reading," for parents, particularly fathers in a divorce situation. In fact, the book is well enough written that it's almost a shame to reserve it only for those people involved in a divorce. Some divorces might not happen, and children in otherwise "stable" marriages might be better off if parents, particularly fathers, took what's written in this book to heart.

JOSEPH R. ZANGA, MD, FAAP,
Maude C. Clarke Professor and Chair, Pediatrics,
Ronald McDonald Children's Hospital of
Loyola University Medical Center, Chicago

. . . not a law book but a font of sage and sensitive advice to noncustodial fathers about how to maintain close and reward-ing relationships with their children after divorce or separation. Drawing on their extensive couseling experience, the authors explain and address the highly emotional and practical issues and the potential roadblocks that such parents may face. It fills a very important niche in the literature on family breakdown.

WALTER WADLINGTON,
James Madison Professor of Law,
University of Virginia

This book is a gem. . . . Indeed, even though it was written for fathers, mothers will also find a treasure trove of sound infor-mation, valuable insights, and frank advice. The authors deal with complicated, often "hot-button" issues with wonderful sensitivity, great humor, and an eagle eye on practicality.

MICHAEL GORDON, PHD,
Professor of Psychiatry, Chief Child Clinical Psychologist,
SUNY Upstate Medical University

WEDNESDAY EVENINGS AND EVERY OTHER WEEKEND

From
DIVORCED DAD
to
COMPETENT CO-PARENT

F. DANIEL MCCLURE PHD

JERRY B. SAFFER PHD

A GUIDE FOR THE NONCUSTODIAL FATHER

THE VAN DOREN COMPANY
CHARLOTTESVILLE, VA.

WEDNESDAY EVENINGS AND EVERY OTHER WEEKEND:
FROM DIVORCED DAD TO COMPETENT CO-PARENT.
A GUIDE FOR THE NONCUSTODIAL FATHER
By F. Daniel McClure, PhD, and Jerry B. Saffer, PhD

Published by THE VAN DOREN COMPANY, 4852 Watts Passage,
Charlottesville, Virginia 22911. 434.975.0238
vandorencompany@earthlink.net

ISBN 0-9679179-8-0

EDITORIAL PRODUCTION: WILLIAM T. VAN DOREN AND LAURA OWEN SUTHERLAND

Publisher's Cataloging-in-Publication
(Provided by Quality Books, Inc.)

McClure, F. Daniel.
      Wednesday evenings and every other weekend : from
divorced dad to comptetent co-parent : a guide for the
noncustodial father / F. Daniel McClure, Jerry B. Saffer.
-- 1st ed.
      p. cm.
      LCCN 00-135554
      ISBN 0-9679179-8-0

      1. Divorced fathers--United States--Psychology.
2. Parenting, Part-time--United States. 3. Children of
divorced parents. 4. Custody of children. 5. Divorce--
United States--Psychological aspects. I. Saffer,
Jerry B. II. Title.

HQ756.M33 2000   306.874'2
                            QBI00-901561

10 9 8 7 6 5 4 3

ACKNOWLEDGMENTS

THIS UNDERTAKING HAS DEMONSTRATED TO US time and time again that we are blessed with a remarkable array of friends and colleagues. Being able to tap their knowledge, expertise, and wisdom has been part of the joy of writing this book. Marion McClure read each and every word of this text on numerous occasions and provided extensive editorial support in the early stages. Thanks to Drs. Vito Perriello, Michael Dickens, and Raymond Ford for their friendship and their expertise in pediatric medicine. Dr. Ronald Heller provided invaluable insights from the perspective of a child psychiatrist. He is a good friend and in our practices we seek his professional expertise early and often. Thanks also to Louise Cole, M.ED., educational specialist, and to Susan Bender, ESQ. for their help and advice. This is a most talented and unselfish group of people, and we thank them.

This work is a testament to the notion that imitation is indeed the most sincere form of flattery. We are greatly indebted to our good friend Michael Gordon, Ph.D., whose prose style we have shamelessly emulated, and whose wit and unique world view we have attempted, albeit in vain, to capture in these pages. Many thanks, Michael.

The authors of this book are relentlessly devoted to minimizing the stress and aggravation in their lives. We have been most fortunate, therefore, to find an editor and publisher who share this same commitment and who, as an added bonus, also just happen to share our love of the national pastime. Bill Van Doren and Laura Owen Sutherland not only handled the technical aspects of their jobs with efficiency and professionalism, they also showed remarkable grace and patience in dealing with two men who color and play with Legos for a living. Their calm temperament and easygoing nature brought joy to a task that easily could have become a nightmare.

Finally, the prerogative of a senior author. When I was young I had the good fortune to observe the work of a most talented and gifted child psychologist. As a technician on the evening shift in a psychiatric hospital, in my spare moments I would pore over his psychological reports, marveling at his empathy and his almost intuitive understanding of the youngsters under his care. The esteem in which I held him ultimately led me to pursue graduate studies myself, and during my training I had the further good fortune to study under him as a mentor. His friendship through the intervening twenty years has truly been a gift, and to co-author this work with him has been an honor. Thank you, Jerry.

Charlottesville, Virginia
November 2000

CONTENTS

PROLOGUE *Saturday Morning* 1

INTRODUCTION 2

1 **TAKING STOCK** *The Death of a Marriage* 7
  Guidelines for Dealing With Your Lawyer 17
  10 Reasons Why a Courtroom Is the Last Place on Earth
  You Want to Find Yourself 20

2 **PLAYING A BAD HAND WELL** *Mourning*............................... 26
  10 Sure Signs That You Haven't Mourned............................... 30
  Mourning's Four Basic Steps.. 34
  A Sure-Fire Recipe for Disaster...................................... 41

3 **PARENTING AS A SKILL** *Becoming Knowledgeable* 44
  Why It Pays to Learn About Child Development 51
  Guidelines for Dealing With Your Child's Therapist................. 63

4 **WHAT DIVORCE DOES TO CHILDREN** *Becoming Aware* 66

5 **DEALING WITH DISCIPLINE** *Becoming Respected*............ 78
  10 Principles of Effective Discipline 84
  Cheap Cliches Worth Remembering 88

  NOT THE REAL QUIZ
  10 Things Guys Don't Always Think About................................ 94

6 **PARENTING AS A RELATIONSHIP** *Becoming Responsive* 97
  10 Things Your Kid Will Quote to His Therapist Someday
  If You're Not Careful.. 102

  THE REAL QUIZ 119

7   **EARNING ACCESS TO
    YOUR CHILD'S WORLD** *Becoming Involved* 122
    10 Ways to Break Your Kid's Heart 130

8   **BRINGING YOUR CHILD
    INTO YOUR WORLD** *Becoming Accessible* 138

9   **MANAGING THE VISITATION** *Becoming Effective* 147
    10 Keys to a "Kid Friendly" Home 149
    Guidelines for Dealing With Pediatricians (Part 1) 163
    "Homework Wars"—10 Ways to Win 169
    Guidelines for Dealing With Your Child's School 172

10 **YOU AND YOUR EX** *Becoming a Gentleman* 179
    Visitation and Your Ex: 10 Keys 190
    The Ten Commandments of Visitation 191

11 **SPECIAL CASES** *Becoming Prepared* 198
    Guidelines for Dealing With Pediatricians (Part 2) 220
    False Accusations of Abuse 225

12 **EYES ON THE PRIZE** *Maintaining Perspective* 242

Afterword: The Blessings of Family 267

PROLOGUE
SATURDAY MORNING

Saturday morning and McDonald's is full. You stop in to get a little breakfast on your way to a soccer game. As you look around, you notice a curious thing. You see a lot of guys with kids . . . not families, just guys with kids. And they look a little uncomfortable—like they don't know exactly what to say or do. They look down at their food. Many eat in silences punctuated by brief questions and even briefer answers. Sometimes just a shrug. Clearly, in many ways these guys feel like strangers to their children—and the feeling is mutual.

Then it dawns on you: These men and their children are having "visitation," the strange and stressful way children and divorced fathers relate. A relationship not occurring naturally, but decreed by some court somewhere. A relationship dictated by a stranger who may or may not ever have seen the child. These guys have made *appointments* to see their children. They picked them up last night. Or this morning. They must have them back at an appointed time. In the meantime, they must try to be fathers—"absent fathers," "noncustodial fathers," "part-time fathers"—whatever. Then they will return their children. They will go home alone and wait for Wednesday evening, perhaps, when they can again see their children at the appointed time.

If you have seen these men, surely your heart goes out to them. If you *are* one of these men, surely your heart aches as you read about yourself.

INTRODUCTION

If you have purchased this book, odds are good you're either in the throes of a pending divorce or in the aftermath of a recent divorce. Either way, you've been through a lot, most likely alone. You've undergone an experience you probably never dreamed would happen to you. One for which you could never have adequately prepared. And one for which there are no role models—and no recipe for success.

This experience has come at a great cost. If you're like most men, it has cost you a great deal of money, and perhaps even your home. It may have cost you your sense of security and the companionship that marriage should provide. If you have become cynical and jaded in the process, it has cost you your idealism. If you have become depressed, it has cost you your sense of well-being. It may have seriously dented your self-respect. Most important of all, you may feel that it has cost you your child.

You have had to give up your role as a full-time, live-in father. It is our fervent hope that this book will help you to better understand and define your new role as a successful and competent part-time parent. In the process, we hope to offer insights, new information, and, the most crucial piece of the puzzle, a new outlook on this, your most challenging new role.

Your new challenge means, first of all, adjusting to a new relationship with the mother of your children. Your challenge is to effectively relate to her in *her* new role as the primary custodian of your children (and as your *former* wife). This is a very tall order, but we want to help you relate to her only as a cooperative and active co-parent of your children.

Our goal is to help you afford your child the best opportunity to fulfill their most important function, which is simply being a kid. Of all the people in the world, you and your ex are in the best position to do this for your children. Judges and attorneys are not. We want to help you maximize your role and minimize theirs.

This is a book for men, about fatherhood. It is designed to provide you with knowledge and support, and to enhance your parenting under these most difficult circumstances. It is difficult at times to be supportive of men without running the risk of being accused of being anti-women. We have no intention of encouraging or entering into "ex-wife bashing." Quite the contrary. We wish to help you work through your anger and to put your marriage relationship into proper perspective—*in the past.* Even though you still have to deal with your ex-wife, the marriage is dead. Gone. We want to help you bury it and let it stay dead.

We, the authors of this book, have a combined experience of over 50 years in the practice of child clinical psychology. This work has brought us a unique set of experiences. In our practices we have seen divorce up close, but with enough distance not to get caught up in the emotional turmoil.

We have conducted formal custody evaluations through the courts, and have witnessed firsthand how ugly, degrading, and damaging such endeavors can be. We have testified on behalf of mothers as well as fathers, and at times we have testified against both mother *and* father. We have worked with parents who were unable to manage their divorce in ways that protected their children, and we have worked with parents who successfully shielded their youngsters from the more damaging aspects of this process.

Most importantly, we have worked day-in and day-out in the business of psychotherapy with children, the overwhelming majority of whom have divorced parents. We have seen too many times how a poorly managed divorce can damage a developing young child. We have also seen how the successful management of issues surrounding a divorce can actually protect a child.

We hope that this book can help you avoid some of the pitfalls now so that you will be in a better position to limit the damage that might result later. Our expertise, such as it is, comes not from scholarly research or academic classes, but from years of clinical experience in the trenches.

If you bought this book out of a love of statistics or hoping to pepper your vocabulary with impressive-sounding jargon and catch-phrases—in other words, psychobabble—we think you'll be disappointed. That's not how we can help you. Instead we offer straightforward observations, anecdotal truths, and, we hope, good common sense.

We have tried to make this an entertaining and readable

guide to help you through this difficult period. We offer specific suggestions, "do's and don'ts," off-the-cuff observations, opinions, and at times just plain random thoughts. Nothing contained herein should be construed as a substitute for counseling, psychotherapy, or specific advice from a qualified mental health, educational, or legal professional. Indeed, we strongly encourage you to seek their counsel and advice early and often.

We also tried to use gender-neutral language and to be as politically correct in our terminology as possible—and it didn't work. We don't know how many children you have, and we don't know if they are sons or daughters. Rather than try to cover all the options, we opted for an easier approach. At times we talked about your "child," at times we talked about your "children." Sometimes we used the masculine, sometimes the feminine. We figured that even if we don't know how many children you have of which gender, *you* do. And that even if we referred to your child as "he," and she's a "she," you would know we really meant "she."

We've organized this book around 12 fundamental themes— 12 steps toward becoming the best father you can be:

1. **TAKING STOCK:** *The Death of a Marriage*
2. **PLAYING A BAD HAND WELL:** *Mourning*
3. **PARENTING AS A SKILL:** *Becoming Knowledgeable*
4. **WHAT DIVORCE DOES TO CHILDREN:** *Becoming Aware*
5. **DEALING WITH DISCIPLINE:** *Becoming Respected*
6. **PARENTING AS A RELATIONSHIP:** *Becoming Responsive*

7. **EARNING ACCESS TO YOUR CHILD'S WORLD:** *Becoming Involved*
8. **BRINGING YOUR CHILD INTO YOUR WORLD:** *Becoming Accessible*
9. **MANAGING THE VISITATION:** *Becoming Effective*
10. **YOU AND YOUR EX:** *Becoming a Gentleman*
11. **SPECIAL CASES:** *Becoming Prepared*
12. **EYES ON THE PRIZE:** *Maintaining Perspective*

In addition, throughout the book, we have asked our friends—professionals in related fields—to help us provide you with more specific information on how to manage the various aspects of your current situation for the ultimate benefit of your child.

A final word. We'll probably tell you a lot of things you've already heard before. There's a good chance you've even heard them from your ex at one time or another. We hope you'll listen to us better than you did to her.

1
TAKING STOCK
The Death of a Marriage

Your moorings have been ripped away. How are you respond-
ing? Are you now a loose cannon, firing blindly at everyone
you believe has wronged you? Are you a ship foundering in a
maelstrom? Are you sinking? Or are you like an experienced
ship's captain, free now to steer your vessel in the direction
most beneficial for you and your crew?

OK, perhaps that's enough nautical imagery. The point is,
you do have the potential to take your ship to a consciously
chosen destination. Your marriage has ended, but you can
still choose to create a life where both you and your children
can thrive. You can do this, but only after you've faced up to
your situation. You can't chart your course if you don't know
your position.

UNCHARTED WATERS

It seems hard to believe now, but there was a time when it was
pretty difficult to get a divorce. Most states had restrictions on
residence, requiring both parties to live alone for as long as a
year before the divorce could be finalized. In many states, having another relationship during that year was considered to be
adultery. There was also a social stigma attached to divorce.

Churches and religious organizations looked down on divorce, and in many quarters it was viewed as a failure to meet personal, social, and parental expectations. These factors tended to give couples pause, and often made them think long and hard over their course of action.

Today, of course, most of the requirements have been relaxed, and the stigma of divorce is minimal, if not gone altogether. It is terribly easy to obtain a divorce, and it is probably no coincidence that the rate of divorce has risen dramatically as sanctions have disappeared.

However, while it has become increasingly easy to *get* a divorce, we as a society have actually done very little to help people *be* divorced. That's the hard part. Divorce has become a more or less easy cruise—right off the edge of the world.

No Map, No Compass, No Landmarks . . . Not Even a Decent Going-Away Party

Throughout the ages, just about every culture has developed rituals to mark the passage from one status or role to another. Many tribal cultures enact elaborate puberty rituals to mark the entry of children into adulthood—bodily scarring and "trials by fire," for example. In other traditions, religious confirmation or the bar mitzvah marks a youngster's transition into adulthood. In our culture, the driver's license often serves this function—not as dramatic as genital mutilation or facial scarring, maybe, but symbolic nonetheless.

Graduations, too, are rites that mark a change in role or status, and they are now staged from kindergarten all the way through college and beyond. In the business world, luncheons or special ceremonies mark promotions, and retirements are marked by formal observances.

And, of course, few rites compare with those celebrating a marriage. First, there is the ritual of engagement or betrothal, with a formal announcement and a ring symbolic of the impending change in status. Then there are the smaller celebrations leading up to the wedding—showers, the bridal registry, the rehearsal dinner, and, of course, the bachelor party. There is a Best Man and a Maid or Matron of Honor, each with specific duties and responsibilities. Parents of the bride and groom are ritually honored, and the bride and groom themselves have a set of very clear expectations and rules to follow. Finally comes the actual wedding ceremony, with great symbolic and ritual significance.

We have rituals for everything from baptism to burial. But not for divorce. If this event is celebrated at all, it is most likely by getting drunk, and probably by getting drunk alone. There is no designation of a Best Man or Maid of Honor to shepherd the couple through this transition. Only lawyers. No culturally determined steps formally mark your progress toward the final moment. No guidelines direct you in your handling of this most important and difficult transition in status.

Most often, in fact, you learn that the divorce has been finalized when you receive a sterile, unceremonious statement from the Court in the mail. It is cold and anonymous, without fanfare or feeling. It does nothing to prepare you for the wellspring of emotion to follow.

Parenthood in divorce may be the most difficult and challenging transition in roles you will ever face. You are no longer married. *But, like it or not, you are also not single.* You are "A Father Who Is Not Married To The Mother Of Your Children" (we still don't know exactly what to call you). And, if you are like most men, you are not the primary caretaker of these children. Your status is . . . . Well, you're in limbo, and there is very little out there to provide you with the knowledge, support, and skills you will need to successfully meet the challenges ahead. You are truly on your own. This is a change in status for which no one can really be adequately prepared.

A Tough Time to Be a Guy

Divorce and shared custody of your children is one of the most difficult situations a man can face, yet there is very little assistance available. You'd think there'd be plenty. After all, we live in a "support group" age. You can hardly pick up the Thursday paper without being overwhelmed by the number of support groups being offered, sometimes for the weirdest things. But odds are you won't find anything for noncustodial fathers. The self-help sections of bookstores are full of good advice on just about any topic you can think of, *except* how to be a divorced, noncustodial father. (Hence this book.)

We live in a time when men are often portrayed in a negative light by the popular culture. Most television dads are depicted as lovable boobs, nice to have around, but not altogether necessary (Bill Cosby was one notable exception from the not too distant past). Many shows that aired in the '50's portrayed fathers as committed, competent, and involved, but today these images are looked down upon as hokey fantasies.

It's acceptable today to be categorically opposed to men in general. Men are routinely portrayed either as violent and psychopathic predators, or simply as idiots or the "Happy Primitive." Surely you've seen the bumper sticker: A WOMAN NEEDS A MAN LIKE A FISH NEEDS A BICYCLE. This can indeed be a tough time to be a guy.

By contrast, the popular media have been celebrating the joys and tribulations of single motherhood for years now through movies, television shows, books, magazines, and even the Internet. You can hardly turn on the TV or open up a magazine without seeing stories about single mothers. These women are almost always portrayed as noble and long-suffering, and at times they seem like candidates for sainthood. (You don't have to read very far between the lines to discover what this says about that stinking, no-good rat who left her in this position.) Even the government worries about single mothers, through numerous policies designed specifically to assist them.

This is as it should be. However, there has been no such interest in single or noncustodial fathers. Society's primary interest in you is to track you down should you become a "Deadbeat Dad" (and they will!). Many critics of these policies claim that they have had the unintended effect of appearing to reduce fatherhood simply to a matter of writing the support check.

Recent trends have combined to promote negative stereotypes about men and fathers, reinforcing the notion that fathers can be dangerous at worst, and inconsequential at best. Either way, these trends suggest that you may indeed be of limited value.

FORGET WHAT YOU HEAR—KIDS NEED FATHERS

These stereotypes are incorrect, of course. While they may make for good drama or political statement, they are wrong. There is overwhelming evidence that the absence of a father in a child's life is perhaps the best single predictor of a negative outcome for that child.

Children without fathers in the home are much more likely to engage in aggressive, anti-social behavior. They are more likely to join gangs and to develop substance abuse problems. Girls are more likely to engage in substance abuse and to become pregnant (and, in a disturbing new trend, to commit violent crimes). Kids who grow up without the active involvement of a father are much more likely to be incarcerated later in life. New and dramatic evidence continues to support the role of strong, competent fathering in the successful future of a child. We are also seeing that this parenting is of value and long-term benefit to the child even if the father does not physically live in the home. Yet the destructive stereotypes about men and fathers persist.

CHILDREN: THE TIES THAT STILL BIND (YOU TO YOUR EX)

We all know that divorce is bad for kids. For lots of reasons. We hear the statistics every time we turn on the news. So many books and articles have been written about this topic, and there will be more. Fortunately, though, we also know enough to be able to anticipate and minimize many of the more serious risks.

Above all, we know one absolute, immutable truth:

CHILDREN OF DIVORCE FARE BETTER IF THEIR PARENTS PUT ASIDE THEIR PETTY SQUABBLES, BEHAVE WITH DIGNITY AND HONOR, AND RESPECT EACH OTHER ENOUGH TO BUILD A WORKING RELATIONSHIP IN THE BEST INTEREST OF THEIR CHILD.

If this is so self-evident, why would we even have to mention it? Well, we won't bore you with the gory details, but you wouldn't believe some of the stuff we've seen as psychologists to the children of divorce. Conflicts over custody and visitation can cause otherwise decent and honorable people to lose all dignity and self-respect. At times they even realize that their behavior would make Jack the Ripper squeamish. But they just can't help themselves. They know they may be doing great harm to their children, but they can't let go. Their hostility, rage, and resentment—their utter hatred for their ex—is just overwhelming. These emotions cloud the otherwise sound judgment of otherwise very caring people.

We have spent hours in therapy with them. We have enlisted the help of their clergy, family members, and friends to help them get perspective. Even their lawyers have counseled them to tone it down, or to moderate their behavior, or not to pursue a particular course of action. But the intensity of the emotions is too great. And they proceed to do untold damage.

They "can't help it." But you *must* help it. You brought a child into this world, and you have a responsibility to see that she receives the full benefit of your best effort at parenting. You

14

may be hurting, and you may be angry and resentful, but your child, not you, is the one with the most to lose.

You and your ex are divorced, most likely for good reasons. You may still have very intense, mixed feelings for her. She may have these feelings for you as well. The two of you may drive each other crazy. But you have a joint obligation that goes far beyond the excess baggage from your failed marriage. Like it or not, your child still binds the two of you together. For a long, long time. Forever, in fact.

We can't control your ex. You can't, either—God knows you've tried, right? Therefore, it's time to give it up. You're divorced now. You don't have to love her, you don't have to respect her, you don't even have to like her. *But you do have to keep your feelings under control and work with her.*

We would all like to think that the two of you could establish an efficient, effective working relationship. But if you could, odds are you'd still be married. So, we can't concern ourselves with her. You can't control her end of things. Managing your own end will be hard enough. You can only conduct yourself as a gentleman, with dignity and self-respect, and hope that she will respond in kind. Either way, you win. If she doesn't respond in kind, you look good by contrast. If she does, then the two of you can go about the business of raising your child. In either instance your child wins, too, because you have modeled excellent behavior for her.

Let's face it, it's over. You guys are rid of each other. Let go of the past and focus on the most important thing of all—your child's well-being. When we say (as we will, over and over) **KEEP YOUR EYES ON THE PRIZE**, this is what we're talking about.

A Courtroom is the Last Place You Want to Find Yourself

If you're already divorced, chances are you've had the opportunity to experience the court system from the inside. If you are a noncustodial or "visiting" father, you've obviously come out on the short end of the proceedings. If your divorce has been particularly contentious, you have had the added benefit of seeing the system at its worst. You've seen it bring out the worst in everyone involved.

You may have heard monstrous things said about you, out loud and in public. Some true, some maybe not so true. No doubt you have responded in kind, or at least wished you could. You have watched in disbelief as the judge makes rulings that seem to defy every grain of common sense in your accumulated experience. You may have watched the two attorneys act like gladiators engaged in mortal combat, only to hear them plan lunch with each other during a recess.

We have no quarrel with the Court or with attorneys. However, our experience is that most people simply don't understand our legal system. We have also seen that the system often doesn't understand them, either.

Our system of law is an entity unto itself. It's based on many confusing and at times contradictory precedents, dictums, and customs, and it employs a very odd language that often only lawyers comprehend. Most people have the mistaken impression that the whole body of law is based on formulations of "right" vs. "wrong," and that therefore it should make sense.

Sorry. It doesn't.

If you watch *Court TV* or any of the talking legal heads on television, you know full well that the law is so squishy that any good attorney can make even the most preposterous interpretations of a law sound plausible. Then the opposing attorney will argue the exact opposite interpretation of the very same law just as convincingly.

This mess is further complicated by the tremendous power and discretion that judges wield in their courtrooms. They enjoy very wide latitude in what they will and will not allow, and they have great discretion in using this power to make decisions. Just like the rest of us, they can be temperamental, inconsistent, self-serving, arbitrary, and even downright cantankerous. But, unlike the rest of us, they hold your future in their hands.

You want, and indeed expect, the judge to be like King Solomon: wise, fair, and consistent. If they were, you believe, they would naturally rule in your favor. When you go into a courtroom, you want the judge to understand your pain, and to appreciate your essential goodness. You want her to have compassion for what you've been through and how you've been misunderstood and slandered. You expect the judge to see through the transparent little games your ex is trying to play, and to empathize with your motives, even when you did stupid things. And you want your attorney, as your representative, to communicate these things effectively to the judge.

Unfortunately, when the judge enters the courtroom, she has a different agenda. *Judge Judy* may seem a cartoon-like exaggeration, but it's not far off. The judge wants the facts. Not excuses, not reasons, not rationalizations, just facts. And

GUIDELINES FOR DEALING WITH
YOUR LAWYER
BY SUSAN BENDER, ESQ., ATTORNEY AT LAW

Do

- tell your attorney of any serious conditions or events affecting your child's health, safety, or well-being. Try to discuss these issues with your ex as well. (**Note:** poor housekeeping is *not* typically a serious health hazard).
- follow your attorney's instructions. If there's something you don't understand, ask.
- keep good records—notebooks, logs, etc. But don't be petty.
- think *at least* twice before calling your attorney at home unless he or she has explicitly told you to do so.
- carefully examine your motives for involving your lawyer in a situation; e.g., is it really a legal issue or simply a power play over your ex?
- above all, **Do What You're Told.** If you're going to pay all of this money for good, sound legal advice and simply ignore it, you might as well save your money.

Don't

- bring your children to the attorney's office unless specifically asked to do so.
- contact your attorney with issues not within the purview of the law.
- contact your attorney to deal with problems you could solve on your own. If your kids are dirty, give them a bath!
- call your attorney just to "vent"—you'll run the risk of being seen as just "crying wolf."
- feel that you always have to speak directly to your attorney. A detailed message is often more efficient, and the paralegal may be able to help you just as well as the attorney.
- above all, don't freelance. Resolve any questions or disagreements with your attorney. If they can't be resolved, get another attorney. But whatever you do, don't be your own attorney.

quickly, too, without a lot of "B.S." She doesn't want to put up with a lot of lip from your attorney, either. She wants the relevant facts presented against a succinct backdrop of legal precedents. Then she wants folks to shut up and let her do her job.

Judges spend most of their time trying to sift through the "spin" that each party puts on the facts. It is probably not uncommon for one of the parties to simply be lying altogether. Even if they don't outright lie, their differing interpretations of the facts can make you dizzy. We've heard each party in a case outline a situation where the facts are absolutely identical. But when you hear their interpretation of these very same facts, you'd think the parties each lived in an alternate universe. That's when they *agree* on the facts.

And everybody has excuses. Everybody has very good reasons for doing very stupid things—and it goes on and on and on. But you know what? The judge doesn't care. She needs specific information, and your feelings and motivations don't matter much. That's why you need a lawyer. They know what the judge needs, and they know how to present it coherently. They try to distill everything you want done into a language and style that the judge can tolerate and digest. Because of this, they don't always present your case the way you would. For this you should be grateful.

It is the rare litigant indeed who leaves the courtroom feeling understood, or feeling that he has had his full and complete say before the bar of justice. The reason is simple. Much of what you feel and have to say simply isn't relevant to the judge's decision.

Similar considerations apply to attorneys. They are paid to represent your interests to the Court. A good attorney will represent your interests aggressively and single-mindedly. Your attorney is paid to listen to your side of the story and represent it to the Court as effectively as possible. He will hold your hand and shepherd you through this ordeal to the end. Your attorney knows that this is perhaps the single most important event in your life—that your emotions are at a fever pitch—and that much of your future hinges on the outcome. Your attorney's job is to balance these considerations against the wants and needs of the law and the judge.

However, don't expect your attorney to have the same emotional investment you do. Don't expect him to buy into your world view. This is his job, what he does for a living. He's done it before, and he will likely still be doing it when your children are grown. The courtroom is a place of conflict. This conflict saps your energy and causes you great anxiety. It is personal to the bone. It hurts. But attorneys go through it every day. They're used to the conflict, and they don't take it personally. Otherwise, they couldn't do it for a living. Even when they aggressively engage the other side in hostile combat, it's not personal. It's their job. They belong to the same local Bar Association; they live and raise their children in the same community; and they may well go up against each other regularly in court. They probably also know the judge personally, as well. Don't expect your attorney to share your anger, resentment, and conviction that your ex is evil personified. Expect him to represent your interests in a competent and professional manner. No more, no less.

10 Reasons Why a Courtroom Is the Last Place on Earth You Want to Find Yourself

1. You'll probably lose.

Face it, the odds are not with you. For a number of reasons—some good, some not so good, the system tends to favor mothers. Public sentiment and tradition are not on your side, and a good attorney can easily exploit these factors to your detriment. You will rarely if ever get the benefit of the doubt, and your motives are apt to be suspect. So, don't whine or complain. Just accept the fact that she is playing from a stronger hand in this situation.

2. Even if you win, you lose.

Too often these situations resemble two prizefighters standing toe to toe, pummeling each other until one falls. While the one left standing "won," the victory came at great cost. In your case, the cost will be mostly to your child.

3. Court is a "Zero Sum" proposition.

Court is an adversarial system, with "winners" and "losers." It's not set up for compromise. It's designed specifically to be adversarial—a high stakes, winner-take-all proposition. But the best interest of the child is never served when one parent "wins" and the other "loses."

4. WHEN YOU ENTER THE COURTROOM,
YOU HAND OVER ALL OF YOUR CONTROL TO THE JUDGE.

Are you sure this is a good idea? By going to Court, you're turn-ing control of your affairs over to a complete stranger. As we discussed, this is also a stranger who plays by different rules than you do—and who is really not very interested in you . . . and who may be having a bad day. The judge's decision is final and over in a flash. There's no arguing the point or lobbying for your cause afterward.

5. JUDGES AREN'T TRAINED FOR THIS.

Judges are attorneys. They went to law school. Maybe they studied psychology in undergraduate school, but they became lawyers. Not psychologists. Not child development experts. Not marriage and family therapists. Not social workers. They're trained in the law, and they think like lawyers. If they thought like psychologists, they'd be one. Even the most sensitive, caring, and intuitive judge still thinks in terms of the law.

6. DO YOU REALLY WANT TO SEND
THE LAWYER'S KIDS THROUGH COLLEGE?

We may sound glib here but, seriously, this stuff can really run into money. Most lawyers don't want to litigate your case. It's a hassle, it's unpredictable, it's aggravating. They would rather settle. But they will go to court if you want them to. It's how they make a living, and they're not cheap. We firmly believe that the money that you work hard for should go toward educating and raising your own child. We have literally seen people spend the equivalent of a college education on petty battles that drag on and on, ultimately serving no one, least of all the child.

7. COURT HEARINGS OFTEN SOW SEEDS OF DISCORD THAT WILL COME BACK TO HAUNT YOU.

Court hurts. It's painful. Often ugly. Things are said that can never be taken back. Accusations are made that will sting for a long time. And you don't have control over the proceedings, remember? Things can quickly take a turn for the ugly, and your zeal to "win" can get in the way of the important things in your life (and especially in your child's life). If you poison the well over a few hours of visitation when your child is six, what's going to happen when your child is 15 and needs the support and help of both parents?

8. EVEN IF YOU "WIN," THERE'S NO GUARANTEE YOU CAN ENFORCE THE SPOILS OF YOUR VICTORY.

Ever heard of a "Show Cause" order? These are petitions people constantly file because they think the other party is operating outside the agreement or court order. When a Show Cause order is filed, a court date is established for some time in the relatively distant future. You then go to Court and one side tells the judge why the other is being unfair and "cheating" on the agreement. The other then either denies this cheating or presents all sorts of reasons why they were driven to cheat by the irresponsible behavior of the other. Typically the judge sends both parties on their way with the instruction to stop cheating and just get along. These orders are very difficult to enforce with any consistency and especially with any speed. They are often flagrantly disobeyed, and only rarely is the offending party called to account. Even when they are, it's simply an official admonition from the Bench to stop doing whatever it is they were doing. Is this starting to sound a little ridiculous?

9. THE CHILD GETS LOST IN THE SHUFFLE.

Each of you is emotionally stirred up. You're angry, outraged. You're defensive, righteously indignant. All of the conflicts in the relationship, the recriminations and accusations and shortcomings and blaming that destroyed the marriage, are played out. If you win, you're vindicated. The Court recognizes that you were right all these years, and that she really was at fault all along. On the other hand, if she should win, it means you really are all of the things she has said you were all these years. Therefore, before you know it, "winning" becomes more important than just about anything else in the world. All of a sudden, then, this is no longer about your child. It's about the failure of your marriage, who's to blame, and essentially who is good and who is not. It becomes personal, and the same old battles are fought out anew, with all of their original emotional intensity. Nowhere in this equation will you find the child's best interest.

10. SEE NUMBER 1.

So what's our advice? The same as always. Learn. Ask questions. Understand what the Court system is for: a last resort for conflict resolution. Going to Court is an admission that the two of you are absolutely incapable of resolving child custody. It signifies the complete breakdown of reason and good faith.

The Court exists for good reasons. It's there to prosecute those who would injure or harm your child. It's there to protect your child from imminent physical, mental, or emotional damage. Not from inconvenience or aggravation, but from *real* danger. Not projected or potential danger that you suspect may occur, but real, *imminent* danger. Too often we expect the Court and attorneys to do things for which they are simply not equipped, and for which the system was not intended. We have seen people go to Court and with a straight face argue about changing custody because one of them sent the kid home repeatedly with dirty laundry.

So, if your child is being placed in real, imminent danger, get to Court as quickly as you can and ask the judge to intervene. Short of that, employ every possible reasonable alternative, such as counseling and mediation, before going to court. Even consider letting the battle go.

If you still decide that Court is the only alternative, stop anyhow and think twice. Sometimes you may come out ahead in the long run if you simply suck it up and let some things go. Don't lose sight of the important in service of the immediate. You should think long and hard before entering a courtroom to resolve issues that you may later come to regard as petty.

We believe that when you are involved in Court you become completely preoccupied. You tend to forget the real business at hand. You have a lot of work to do, and the chances of success are much greater if you can avoid repeated court battles. So, forget about court and let's get busy.

2
PLAYING
A BAD HAND WELL
Mourning

There are two kinds of hands even the worst poker players love. The first is four aces. Any damn fool can play that hand. The second is a hand without even a high card in it. That one is also easy. Get out!

But most hands fall somewhere in the middle, and the truly great poker players know how to play them. They can take a few good cards and a few lousy cards and make a winner out of it. This is poker creativity, and the poker gods shine upon such players.

The hand you must play is also in the middle. You have great cards, because you have kids you can love and a way to support them. You have a few lousy cards, including an angry ex-wife, whose anger at you may even be fueled by a new lover. And you have some so-so cards, in that you don't see your children on a daily basis and therefore don't know their day-to-day life. We say "so-so," because while you may have been home for breakfast every day and dinner most nights when you were married, if you're like most dads, seldom were you home or with your child in the middle of the day.

Our wish for you is to play these middling cards well. These are the ones that are going to make or break you as a divorced father. We have learned a great deal from our patients, many of whom have been dealt truly lousy cards. We have great respect, as well as a soft spot in our hearts, for those who can take a bad hand and play it well. Our wish is that you play these cards like a competent old pro. We hope that someday you will master the art of living with a hand containing a mad ex, her self-righteous spouse, and a child you are not saying goodnight to on a regular basis—and do it with style, grace, and aplomb.

This Probably Isn't How You Planned On Spending the Rest of Your Life

Let's face it, this isn't what you planned on when you decided to marry and have children. We all know the statistics on divorce in this country. No doubt you were aware of these when you decided to marry. Perhaps others even talked to you about this. But no one who falls in love and plans to marry thinks they'll end up divorced (except maybe in Hollywood). No one enters into marriage with the notion that it won't last.

No, if you're like most men, you fell in love and decided on marriage with full faith and conviction that *your* relationship would be different. *Your* relationship would survive the stresses and pressures that doomed others. You believed your relationship was special, somehow immune from these difficulties.

28

Sitting where you are now, after the pain and agony you've been through, it may be hard to remember the hopes and dreams that you and your bride shared when you wed.

Even more important, though, is that when you decided to have children, you did not do so with the notion of being a "part-time dad." You didn't plan on raising your children with limited access to them. Having to share their precious care and rearing with someone you can't get along with. Having to drive across town on a rainy day to pick them up from a woman who has little use for you—then returning them to her and going home alone. Not being able to contribute to their moral and spiritual development the way you had hoped. And, perhaps most disturbingly, possibly sharing them with another man, having them become attached to a stepfather.

No, if you're like the rest of us, you entered into marriage and fatherhood with a wealth of hopes, dreams, and wishes for the future. And you shared them with your wife. Our guess is that nowhere among these aspirations would we find the fantasy of being alone and not having complete access to your own children. You saw yourself as a man surrounded by his family, eating popcorn and watching videos, tucking the kids in their beds when the movie was over. A family outing to watch your oldest play in a soccer tournament. Going on vacations with other families. You saw yourself as a successful husband and father, able to meet the needs of your family, those who depend on you for nurturance, guidance, and support.

Even under the best of circumstances, divorce shatters

these fantasies. You may maintain a civil relationship with your ex, and you may see a great deal of your children. You may even believe that the divorce was in the best interests of the children and that in fact you are all better off. No matter, it will never be the same. There will be no Sunday evenings spent with the family in front of the TV. Science projects and term papers will be done without your help. Soccer games will likely cause anxiety because your ex or former friends will be there. You may have to fight tooth and nail just to get information from the school or from the doctor. Family vacations will never be the same. Things have changed forever. Not just for you, but for your children.

Times will be tough, but they can also be rewarding.

You Can and Will Be a Competent, Effective, and Influential Father

There are some things you have to do, and they're not a lot of fun. Mourning is first and foremost among them.

If you refuse to mourn, you cannot go forward. You're stuck. And when you're stuck, you end up fighting the same battles of the marriage all over again. Except that you tend to fight them in court, which is really not a good idea (see Chapter 1). To get on with the task of parenting your children and having a "successful" divorce, you must first conduct some soul-searching and give up some things that you have held dear for a very long time.

It's time to mourn.

10 SURE SIGNS THAT YOU HAVEN'T MOURNED

1. IF YOU FEEL ANGRY MORE OFTEN THAN YOU FEEL SAD.
2. IF YOU NEED TO NUMB YOURSELF WITH:
   DRUGS
   ALCOHOL
   SEX
   FOOD
   . . . OR ANYTHING ELSE
3. IF YOU DON'T GIVE A DAMN ABOUT ANYTHING.
4. IF YOU GIVE TOO MUCH OF A DAMN ABOUT *EVERYTHING*.
5. IF YOU CAN'T STAND BEING ALONE.
6. IF YOU WANT TO CALL UP YOUR EX JUST TO HANG UP ON HER.
7. IF YOU REFUSE TO GO PLACES BECAUSE YOUR EX MIGHT BE THERE.
8. IF YOU SEE YOUR EX'S INFLUENCE IN EVERYTHING YOUR KID DOES.
9. IF YOU SEE YOUR EX IN YOUR DREAMS, BUT THESE DREAMS ARE NIGHTMARES.
10. IF YOU THINK ABOUT YOUR EX MORE THAN YOU THINK ABOUT YOUR KIDS.

FACING THE VOID: THE TASK OF MOURNING

The questions are all too familiar:

"Am I a failure?"

"Am I destined to become a minor figure in my child's life?"

WEDNESDAY EVENINGS ....

"Am I going to live the rest of my life frustrated over the loss of influence with my own children?"

These are the questions we hear from men in your position. The answers are not easy, but they all have one thing in common. You have assumed a role for which you have never trained. You are (take your pick):

- "Noncustodial Father"
- "Absent Father"
- "Part-Time Father"
- "Divorced Father"
- "Visiting Father"

You can choose any one of these, but we reject them all. *Your new role is that of "co-parent" to your child.* And our mission is to help you adopt this role in an active, positive, and enthusiastic way.

But this is not your first task. Before you can adopt this new and challenging role, you need to do the depressing stuff.

Many people will tell you that you have to mourn the loss of your marriage in order to go on with your life. And you will try to keep a straight face. If you're like a lot of men, you believe that you finished mourning before the divorce was even final. You had lots of time to prepare for the death of your marriage, and you thought about it a lot. But trust us, you didn't really mourn. You simply got used to the idea of getting a divorce.

Consider what happens with the mourning for someone who dies. For example, you may have had a relative or loved one who died from a long, extended illness. Everyone knew the disease was terminal, and expected the person to die. Often the physicians have even notified the family that the patient is not expected to live through the month, or through the week. Everyone knew the end was coming. They talked about it. They made the proper arrangements and were fully prepared.

Until it happened.

And then they fell apart. In spite of all the preparation and *thinking* about the impending loss, they simply weren't ready for the emotional blow. Because you can't really deal with a situation on an emotional level until it *happens*.

You can't really mourn the loss of your marriage until you are divorced. You may have thought about it a lot, even with a sense of resignation or perhaps even relief. You decided it was the right thing to do under the circumstances, and it may have even made perfect sense. But then it actually happened. Now it's time to mourn. You're not just mourning the loss of your marriage. You're also forced to give up a number of images of *yourself* that you may not have even realized you had.

Images, What Images?

The first task is to say goodbye to what you have dreamed of for years, even though you may have been unaware of it. Your image of yourself as being an ideal husband. Competent, capable, loved, and yes, maybe even adored. Your image of yourself in your own home, surrounded by your family who needs you and who looks to you for strength and guidance. Your image of yourself as a competent and involved father, adored by his children.

It may sound odd to think about giving up *images* of yourself, but that's because you're not a shrink. Bear with us.

Think about it. If you asked even very young children how they would see themselves as a father and husband, they might first look at you like you were crazy. But then they would proceed to rattle off in surprising detail their individual notions of the fathers and husbands they will one day become. Their images would be comprised of a number of their experiences with important men, such as their own fathers, coaches, doctors, sports figures, and, unfortunately, even TV fathers.

These images are formed very early, and they become an important part of us. Long before these adult roles become real, idealized images of how they will come about have formed. We want you to understand their power. You will begin to feel how powerful they are when you try to give them up. They've been with you far longer than either your wife or your children.

Mourning is never easy or without pain. But *completing* the process of mourning is much easier in the event of actual death or permanent loss. In death, ceremonies and rituals assist in the process, and people come together and support one another. You know that the person is gone forever. Although it's painful, you put them to rest, mourn the loss, and go on.

Not so with divorce. Nobody died, only the marriage. There's no formal ceremony, and nothing physical to be buried. And while divorce may sound final, if you have children, it's not an ending at all—it's just the beginning of a new phase. Not only must you continue to deal with your ex-spouse, but these dealings will often be unsatisfying and full of conflict. You will have to conduct the very important business of raising your child in an atmosphere that may be contaminated by irritation and aggravation. You will have to do this largely on your own.

34

There aren't many things we know for sure, but one thing we do know is that if you never mourn, your odds of success are just about nil.

These are not the kinds of things guys typically discuss over a beer or during a round of golf. But these images must be mourned and put away, just as if they were dead. If you never say good-bye to them you will never be able to construct the new images essential to your new role. You will be in constant denial. You will be looking for new ways to express the same old things, putting old wine into new bottles.

Your task is to give up these old images. Here's how.

Mourning's Four Basic Steps

1. Take Inventory

We're talking about *emotional* inventory, the kind that hurts. The kind that we never do until we're in deep . . . uh . . . trouble.

- Sit. Think. Be still. Listen. Try to face these images of yourself as a father and as a husband. Think about the people who helped create these images for you: your father—your grandfather—an uncle—a family friend. Think about the ways you admired them—the ways you wanted to be admired by your own children, and by your wife.
- Open yourself up. This basically means, listen to people. Try to get a sense of where things went wrong. Try to understand your part in the death of your marriage. Yeah, we know, we know—she did a lot of stuff. But so

did you. You probably didn't handle the things that she did very well, either. So try to let down the defenses and take an honest look.

- Find an honest friend. Talk to him or her. More importantly, *listen* to him or her. If you don't have such a friend, you're in more trouble than you thought: Do your best to find or make or rediscover an honest friend.

2. BEGIN THE PROCESS

- Treat yourself as you would treat someone in mourning. Would you be frantic and demanding with someone going through the throes of mourning? Would you neglect someone in mourning? Would you be impatient and hurry them along? No. So give yourself the same strength that you would offer to others.
- Would you tell someone in mourning not to cry? Or to stop feeling sorry for himself? Of course not. Would you encourage him to seek the support of friends? Or allow some small indulgences? Of course you would. Be kind to yourself, but don't let yourself off the hook, either.
- Learn something about yourself. When you are in a relationship, do you tend to treat a woman as a possession? Are you demanding and selfish? Do you expect more than you're willing to give? Does your ego get in the way of cooperation? Or are you passive, a dishrag? Do you give as much respect as you demand? Resolving these issues is clutch if you ever want to have a successful relationship.

- Examine these issues in relation to the sexual aspects of your relationships. Next to money, sexual problems lead the list of concerns among divorced couples. Consider the possibility that you may be a lousy lover—a selfish or demanding lover—or a disrespectful lover. Learn how to talk about these issues with both men and women.

3. GUILT AND ANGER

- Take stock of your present emotional state. Do you feel guilty? Do you feel that you have forever damaged your children? These emotions will be crucial for you to explore. We're not telling you not to feel guilty. We're telling you to manage your guilt like a big boy and learn something from your mistakes.
- Are you angry and hostile? Is rage dominating your thinking? Do you feel you've been betrayed by the one person you thought you could trust and depend on?—the one person to whom you showed your vulnerabilities? Do you find yourself waking up in the morning cursing lawyers and judges? God knows, we're not telling you that you shouldn't be angry. But this is *your* anger. You need to manage it in ways that won't be destructive to your children. (Anger at lawyers . . . well, we can't help you there.)

4. FINISHING TOUCHES

- Do you need therapy? Do you and your child need to go to counseling? Don't be afraid to seek professional help. Again, would you tell a friend in mourning not to go to a support group, a bereavement group, or a trained professional? We hope not. And you shouldn't be afraid to use these sources of support, either. This is a big job you've undertaken, and a most important one. It's a lot to ask a man to do on his own.

- Finally, start examining your images of yourself in light of your new role, your role as an active, involved co-parent to your children. We hope we'll be able to help you do this, and to create a new life for yourself, centering around your new relationships with your children and former spouse, and keeping your eyes on the prize.

FILLING THE VOID: RETHINKING YOUR ROLE AS A PARENT

We hope that as you go through the mourning process you will begin to develop new conceptions of yourself as a father to your children. These conceptions will revolve around confidence and strength rather than conflict and anxiety. Once you have mourned the loss of the marriage, you can begin to construct a successful divorce. You are in a position of appropriate distance from the intense emotional baggage of the marriage. You are able to clear your head and begin to view things more objectively. And you have the freedom to reconstruct your role as father, the most important man in your child's life.

Up til now your parenting has probably been clouded, even contaminated, by the dysfunction in the marriage. You have had to parent under very adverse circumstances. If you're like most people, the problems in your marriage didn't just arise six months before the separation. No, they've been festering all along, and probably worsened after children came along. They have profoundly colored life within the home.

You have had to father your child in an atmosphere of conflict, stress, and anxiety—or even in the face of open hostility and active attempts to undermine your role. As you no doubt know, parenting often becomes the battleground for conflicts that have nothing to do with the child. For example, if your wife is angry and resentful that you spend all of your time and energy in pursuits outside the home, she is more apt to undermine your attempts to exert your influence when you are home. If you are engaged in sexual power struggles with her in the bedroom, do you seriously think you're going to support her when she disciplines your son for speaking disrespectfully to her?

Even under the best of circumstances, even when parents agree on virtually every aspect of parenting, any conflict within the marriage tends to prevent them from supporting each other's attempts at parenting. Your situation has been much worse than that. Things have indeed been very tough.

Tough for your child, too. Think about it from her perspective. She's been parented in an atmosphere of stress, conflict, and anxiety. She's probably seen both of you acting openly hostile, undermining each other. She may have learned how to capitalize on the dysfunction, or she may have been frozen and immobilized by it. Either way, you can bet she's been affected.

She's experienced conflicts of her own over the inability of her parents to construct a successful marriage. Conflicts over "who's right and who's wrong"—when there *is* no "right" or "wrong." Her attachments have been threatened, her sense of security has been shaken. One result: it has doubtless made her a more difficult child to parent. It has hurt your standing with her as well. She has not always seen you at your best. She has seen you as a source of conflict in the home. She's seen you under very adverse conditions. She may have heard things about you that no man would wish for his child to hear. And she has likely seen your authority and position with her undermined.

But all of that should be behind you now. If you're looking for some positive aspects of the divorce, this is one. Now you can parent from a position of strength. Your emotional state will be different, because you're not constantly arguing or giving someone the cold shoulder. Or avoiding contact. Or instigating conflict. You will be less defensive and less angry. You will be less conflicted. Your emotional life is now free from these things that sap your strength and immobilize you. Now you can have more energy, more focus.

Now you can also view your child's behavior more objectively—not as an outgrowth of her mother's failures or shortcomings. Not through the filter of your own guilt or anger—and without ulterior motives relative to you versus her mother.

But you're not the only one who's free. Everything we've said about you is relevant to your ex, too. She too may now be in a much better position to act as an effective mother to her child. She is also free now to parent her child in an atmosphere of less conflict, hostility, and defensiveness. Let's face it, you may have been a lousy husband. Your marriage may have been played out like a country music song. But this doesn't mean you can't be a dynamite dad.

She may not have been such a bargain as a wife, either—but she can still be a great mother. Don't fall into the trap of assuming that she will treat the children in the same way she treated you, or with the same motives. The relationship, the attachments, the emotions, and the power distribution are all vastly different. One of the major things that you need to work through is to allow her to be a great mother. She's now a single parent for the first time, too, you know.

Finally, your child is now free. She is free from living in that same contaminated atmosphere. She may be sad. She may be experiencing her own mourning process. She may be having loyalty conflicts and all the things we know kids go through in divorce. But the air she breathes has also been cleansed by the divorce. She's no longer living in the midst of your collective dysfunction. She no longer has to see you as a party to the conflict, or as its source—or as a failed husband, disrespected or devalued by her mother. She can now see you in a whole new light: as a competent, confident, secure father—someone solid she can depend on for support, security, and love. Is there any better gift you could give her?

In the sections to follow, we will give you the steps you must follow, to do this for her. Meanwhile, we leave you with this cautionary formula:

A Sure-Fire Recipe For Disaster

Step 1

Take a man who is unable to undertake a good, honest self-examination. Make sure that he will not look at his own shortcomings, and that he is unwilling to risk mourning his own idealized images of himself as husband and father.

Step 2

Mix in approximately one metric ton of defensiveness. This defensiveness can be triggered by any of a number of ingredients. A hostile ex-spouse; a "zero-sum" mentality brought about by close contact with lawyers and Court personnel; fear of mourning (see Step 1); or any combination of the above.

Step 3

Allow mixture to gel. You'll know the process is complete when the man shows a clear conviction that none of the difficulties in the marriage are his fault. A most remarkable transformation takes place at this point. The most obvious sign: the woman he once loved becomes the wife he always loathed, who then becomes the flesh-eating, blood-sucking piranha with whom he must now share the parenting of his children.

Step 4

In order to reach its full size, this mixture must be leavened with others who will support it. These must be people who are also willing to deny enough reality to adopt your world view.

(Warning! Anyone willing to adopt this distorted world view is bound to have problems of their own, which *they* are working out through *you*. No matter, though, you won't notice. You'll be as blind to their difficulties as they are to yours. Having a common enemy will be all you need to "bond" the mixture at this point.)

Step 5

The bonding effect of the "common enemy" mentality will ultimately override common sense. When you find someone who shares your world view, and bond with them over a common enemy, you will mistake this for love.

Step 6

At this point the odds are that you will choose to affiliate yourself with this person, thereby creating an instant replay of your initial relationship.

Step 7

Congratulations! Your denial of your own difficulties—mixed with willing accomplices who have their own axes to grind—has created a bona fide disaster. (Caution: Enjoy it while it lasts, which won't be long. This recipe goes bad quickly. But don't worry. If you still refuse to complete your mourning, you can recreate it any number of times over the course of your lifetime.)

This recipe is quick, easy, and can be made in lots of variations. While many substitutions can be made for various ingredients, the recipe's foundation is always denial and refusal to mourn. For adults only. Children starve on this diet.

3

PARENTING
AS A SKILL
Becoming Knowledgeable

Airline pilots don't need to be mapmakers, but their complex job requires that they know how to use a map. Your job as a father is tough enough—no one expects you to become an expert in child development. But much about the course you will follow has been charted. A great deal is known about parenting and child development. You can learn about the stages you and your child will be going through, and how you can be of help. We men have been accused of resisting, at all costs, seeking directions, even in a place new to us. But if you're reading this book, you're already using a map. The more you know, the stronger you can be as a father. Learning about your child's development can be enjoyable and can give you a sense of accomplishment and confidence. Going through the brambles of parenting is easier when you know where you're headed.

Two facts should guide your parenting. First, parenting is an investment—the most serious investment you'll ever make.

Would you buy stocks without learning all you could about the market or at least reading a prospectus? No. Simply put, this would be bad business. No matter how intuitive or lucky you are in business, developing and mastering basic knowledge and skills will make you a better investor. As with investing, parenting is a set of skills that can be learned and perfected.

A second guiding fact is that the fruits of parenting are often not readily apparent. Sure, you enjoy your children, and there is much love shared between you. But there are lousy parents who love their children just as much. You can enjoy your children and have lots of fun without actively parenting them. You can't always immediately see the difference between good and bad parenting.

Active parenting is hard work. Active parenting requires vigilance, effort, and perseverance. Even at its best it will bring a measure of pain and heartache. In your circumstances it will be even harder. You do not have the luxury of parenting full-time. Worse, there may be those who at best will not support your parenting, and who at worst will attempt to undermine it. You will have an even harder time realizing the fruits of your labors, because your time with your children is limited.

Parenting will require a degree of maturity on your part that you may never have anticipated needing. It will call on an inner strength that you may never have thought you had. Unlike planting a garden or building a house, you won't be able to measure your progress each day. For sure, you will receive "dividends" along the way. But most likely you won't truly know what kind of job you've done until it's over.

If you think about it, a lot of what we do is geared toward an expected payoff at some later date. If you exercise on a regular basis, odds are it is not because you simply love to sweat. And we know that you don't always feel better afterward. It's because you know your life will be better down the road as a result. If you salt away a little money every payday, it's not because you don't really need or want it now. There are lots of things you could spend it on. But you're anticipating a payoff later.

The payoff for active, effective parenting is a well-adjusted, productive member of society, capable of good relationships and possessing a range of competencies that aid in that adjustment. Obviously, you are not going to see this in your eight-year-old. And you can bet the ranch you won't see it in your 15-year-old. This is a long-term project you've signed up for.

Just like everything else, parenting is a skill. Better put, it's a series of skills. Just like other skills, parenting skills can be applied marginally, with little forethought and practice, or they can be studied, practiced, and mastered. Many fathers fall into the trap of believing that parenting is "intuitive," something you're just supposed to come by naturally. Something you're just expected to do, sort of like continuous on-the-job training. These guys have the misguided notion that they are already supposed to know how to do this stuff. This makes it hard for them to seek information or even admit that there are things they just don't know.

But this is wrong. Your only real experience of parenting is that which you yourself experienced. Even under the best of circumstances, your parents surely made mistakes. If you don't master the skills of being a father, you will simply be parenting your child in the same way you were parented. Or worse, you'll try to parent your children exactly *opposite* from the way you were parented. Big mistake. Common sense tells us that there are major differences between children, between situations, and that a host of factors influence our parenting decisions. This is why you need to base your parenting style on a bedrock of basic skills.

Great fathers are made, not born. There is no great mystery to parenting. A specific set of skills must be mastered. A knowledge of the fundamentals of child development. Knowledge of sound disciplinary techniques. An understanding of what specific dangers divorce presents to children. And a body of common-sense truths that women perhaps know intuitively, but which seem to escape men. This is a basic core of competency that can be understood and mastered.

Once you have these skills and this core knowledge, you are prepared for the *art* of parenting. The art of parenting involves applying this knowledge and these skills in a flexible, enthusiastic, and caring way, so that your child's development can unfold in a free and healthy manner. Flexibility, empathy, and a good sense of timing are not enough, though. You have to have the basic skills first.

In acquiring and applying these skills, four principles serve as guideposts:

1. FOCUS. You must focus on the task. Your focus cannot be clouded by anger and resentment. Your focus cannot be clouded by competition with your ex or preoccupation with work. You must be free to learn and to apply what you learn without these toxic distractions.

2. COMMITMENT. You must be willing to put aside any thought, any activity, or any intrusion that will steer you away from your task. You must possess a dog-like tenacity in your quest to become absolutely the best father you can be. There is no substitute for commitment.

3. HONESTY. You must be willing to say out loud that you don't know. You are not an expert in child rearing yet, and you must be as open to seeking instruction as you can possibly be. You will be parenting in a vacuum much of the time. You will be parenting in the absence of credible feedback. And you will be parenting under very stressful circumstances. You will make mistakes, and there will be things that you simply do not know. Acknowledge this, hold your head up, and keep on plugging away.

4. FAITH. Finally, you must absolutely believe that you will succeed. Lack of faith in yourself will become your greatest enemy if you let it. You must believe that, in spite of your circumstances, you will become a great dad. You owe it to yourself and to your child. No matter how much money you make, how many awards you receive, or how many trophies you can accumulate, this is the most important job you will ever have. Give it everything it deserves.

(((

FOUR GUYS IN NEED OF SOME ANSWERS

THE PHONE RINGS. IT'S DAVE. He's been having difficulty with his ex—again. Dave has a three-year-old daughter, Amy. He and his ex have had a terrible divorce, even worse than their marriage, and that's really saying something. Tonight Dave is enraged. In the past three or four weeks, every time he goes to Amy she clings desperately to his ex, crying. He's beginning to see a "pattern" now, he says, and he's hot. He's convinced his wife is putting the child up to it, "brainwashing" her into being afraid of him. For her part, the ex is somewhat suspicious of Dave, wondering aloud why the child would be so fearful, what Dave could possibly have done to cause this.

Then there's Tony, who's in trouble for disciplining his five-year-old so much. He can't understand why this kid keeps wetting the bed. He's doubly frustrated that the kid doesn't respond to punishment. This kid has been trained, he's been "dry" for almost two years.

Then Keith is broken-hearted because his nine-year-old daughter would rather spend the night with a friend on "his" night. All of a sudden she wants to bring friends to his house on "his" visitation time. Even when he went to the family reunion, she wanted to bring a friend with her.

Finally, Robert. Robert just filed a Show Cause order against his ex, who refuses to let their seven-year-old fly to Utah over Christmas break without accompaniment. It's 2,000 miles and two connecting flights, but he's heard that flight attendants are very helpful in these situations.

What do these guys have in common? They all have something to learn about children.

Dave needs to understand that it's normal for three-year-olds to develop separation anxiety and cling to the mother, particularly when they experience stress. If Dave was aware of this, he might not automatically presume that his ex has put the child up to this.

And Tony. Tony needs to understand that even when five-year-olds have been fully toilet trained for some time, they may briefly revert to bedwetting for no particular reason. Under stress, kids may revert to earlier behaviors, and the first to re-emerge is often bedwetting. The kid doesn't respond to punishment because his behavior isn't willful. It's developmental.

For Keith's part, he needs to know that, at his daughter's age, the developmental challenge is to begin to loosen the intense ties to the parents and begin to develop peer-group affiliations. This helps the child in the early stages of establishing her own identity.

And poor Robert—what can we say? It is simply beyond a seven-year-old's wherewithal to manage the task he's foisting on his daughter. Even if the flight attendants attend to her physical needs, this trip is far beyond her emotional capacity at seven.

IN CHILD DEVELOPMENT (AS IN ALL ELSE), KNOWLEDGE IS POWER

The more you know about child development, the greater the impact you will have on your child. Because you will understand him better. And if you understand him better, you can know what to expect and how to anticipate situations proactively.

An understanding of child development is crucial to effective parenting, particularly if you are a noncustodial parent. As a "part-time parent," you probably don't meet with the play group at the park three times per week. Or volunteer at the school the other two days. Or participate in the co-op daycare program.

WHY IT PAYS TO LEARN ABOUT CHILD DEVELOPMENT

1
You'll have a better idea what to expect
from your youngster at various ages.
2
You'll be able to anticipate developmental shifts.
3
You'll be prepared for the emotional changes
your child goes through.
4
You will be better able to meet your child's
emotional needs.
5
You'll get your feelings hurt less.
6
You'll be better able to identify any problems.
7
You'll blame your ex less.
8
You won't call your attorney so often.
9
You'll better understand your child.
10
Your child will feel understood.

Unless you're a coach, a teacher, or a daycare worker, you probably don't have much exposure to children. This makes it hard to have a solid frame of reference as to what's normal and what's not. We would never suggest that you compare your youngster to others. However, contact with other children does give you a sense of what's "normal"—a frame of reference against which to evaluate your child's behaviors, needs, and developmental progression. Each child is certainly unique, but children do go through normal developmental stages that are pretty stable and predictable. Familiarizing yourself with these developmental paradigms will help you in a number of ways (see box on page 51).

We don't want to teach you a course in child development. We do want you to be aware of your child's changing needs, skills, and abilities as he develops.

We are going to roughly outline what to expect at differing ages, but keep in mind that the specific ages are in no way rigid or fixed. Use these ages as guidelines. Our aim is to highlight the most important developmental tasks facing your child, then outline your job in coming to grips with these challenges. Later we deal with many of these issues in more depth.

AGE 0–6 MONTHS
YOUR CHILD'S DEVELOPMENT

Children come into the world helpless. They mainly eat, sleep, and poop. What they need now is to feel safe, warm, secure, and nourished.

At around two months your child begins to smile to a familiar face, and shortly thereafter he'll make sounds and "coo" in ways that you will come to know mean different things.

During this period the primary attachment is to mom, for obvious reasons. This attachment bond will be crucial to later development. As the child grows older, "secondary attachments" become more and more important.

Your Job

Hold your child and rock him. Feed him when possible. Attempt to clear your mind of everything else but what you are doing at that very moment. Support the other care-givers, even if they may have little use for you. Accept the fact that your role is rather limited at this point, and take comfort in the indisputable fact that it is important.

Babies are scary. But they tolerate mistakes pretty well. Don't pawn your child off on others just because he scares you. Get used to him. You're not a real father until you have a yellow stain on your shoulder and baby poop under your fingernails. Relax, nobody ever died from this stuff.

Also, babies don't give much back, they're just not made that way. They're demanding, and they take. He'll give plenty later.

6–12 Months
Your Child's Development

During this time your child is doing some remarkable things. He will clearly recognize people, and he will begin to say a few recognizable sounds that eventually will turn into words. He is able to communicate his needs better, and he can understand some communications from you. He is filled with awe and wonder, and he continues to do things that are tailor-made to make adults love him and care for him. Make sure you're around enough to be a part of this. (Your child is also teething, which will make him cranky for no apparent reason, and he'll be fussy at unpredictable times, because it hurts. There are a number of preparations in drug stores that can be applied to soothe his gums.)

Around 12 months he will begin to make tentative attempts at walking, and he will be curious in the extreme.

Your Job

Your imperative at this point is tolerance and patience. Realize that the chances of his saying "MaMa" at this point far outweigh those of his saying "DaDa." Don't interpret this as rejection. Also, during this period youngsters begin to show "stranger anxiety." This is a crying response when the primary attachment figure (guess who) is out of their sight. Don't mistake this very normal response for a deliberate rejection of you. And don't let others misinterpret this crying as having something to do with you. This is a very normal response, and the child very quickly recovers with gentle soothing and distracting play.

During this time there are very specific types of toys and other materials that you must have and make available to him. When you have him in your care make sure you have enough energy and materials to keep him appropriately stimulated and entertained. Pay close attention to his physical needs. And above, all, handle transitions between your care and your ex's carefully. It will be hard for you to give him back, and you have to deal with this with patience and dignity.

1–3 Years
Your Child's Development

This is when things really start to take off. The child will typically begin to walk at around 12–14 months, first "cruising" by holding on to furniture and moving sideways, and then by taking actual steps.

As you might imagine, this opens up a whole new world of wonder to the child, with all sorts of places and things to explore. As mobility increases, so does the child's sense of power.

The child gradually begins to get an awareness that he is a separate individual. Separate from the environment and separate from those in it. He begins to learn that he can influence the environment as well—by making his wishes clearly known, and by making his upsets clearly known. He also learns that he can influence the environment by simply resisting, saying "no." Welcome to the Terrible Two's.

In the latter part of this stage, toilet training becomes a major developmental task, and it usually coincides with major developments in communication ability.

Your Job

This is when the child begins to give back, and you are re-warded for your patience earlier. Kids at this age really begin to show their individual personality, and it is a joy to behold. They are exuberant, enthusiastic, carefree, and into everything.

If sleep deprivation characterized your adjustment to your child's first year, total exhaustion is the hallmark of this phase. Studies have had grown-ups follow two-year-olds around all day and imitate their activities. And they can't do it. They can barely last a full morning. The kids can go on forever.

Play with your child. Put everything out of your mind but what you are doing with him at that moment. Read to him. Keep him stimulated, and enjoy his mobility, but protect him. Safety is a major concern at this point, and your home should reflect these concerns. He will need a nap whether he wants one or not. Don't let your need to have more time with him deprive him of a nap. Not only will your ex be furious, but you will keep him from rest that he vitally needs. Make sure that your routine is consistent with his mother's, particularly in terms of the toilet training.

3–5 Years
Your Child's Development

He now walks and runs with the best of them, so hold on and fasten your seat belt. He will now turn into the Great Explorer, excited by all things new, and confident that he can find his way home. Preschool is a new source of excitement, with new social experiences and the first real experience of structure. Play will be vigorous and full-tilt. She will be learning a number of skills: playing hard without being out of control; independence without defiance; the joy of cooperation. She will amaze you with her absolute enthusiasm over the simplest of things.

Your Job

You need to help your child feel powerful and accomplished. It's important for you to be able to allow her to venture out into her environment without being overprotective. Encourage his independence, but be there for him when he needs you. Share in the excitement and unbridled enthusiasm of new discovery.

Allow her to be more interested in neighborhood kids or pre-school friends than she is in you. Be there when she needs you, but encourage her attempts at socialization with others. You will also be an active *teacher* of social interactions, as you will participate more and more in his play. You will teach him to adapt his behavior to different rule-structures. And you will be teaching him a lot by the way you deal with his mother.

5–7 YEARS
YOUR CHILD'S DEVELOPMENT

This is a time when boys attempt to be the "man of the house" and girls try to be the "woman of the house." They are beginning to develop sex-role identifications, and, despite what some people may tell you, there *are* differences between boys and girls. They are both terribly sexist, and competition is the name of the game: competition with each other, competition with you, and competition with their mother.

Rules are very important during this time. The games that children are attracted to during this period are highly rule-governed. They teach the child that *all* activities in our society are rule-governed. Children in this stage tend to see the world in black-and-white terms.

Formal schooling begins at this time. Much of early schooling reinforces rule structures as well.

Children are beginning to form attachments outside of the nuclear family, and their age-mates are becoming increasingly important to them.

Your Job

If you have done your job right, by this point you are a major figure in your child's life. He sees you as a dependable, supportive, and nurturing man, one after whom he can pattern himself. Your daughter sees you in the same way, and will use you as a model against which to judge other men.

In this period your son will constantly behave in ways that may challenge your authority (in his bid to be "man of the house"). Your job is to see this for what it is and to avoid the temptation to respond in kind. You don't need to defeat this kid. You need to provide firm, consistent limits. Your daughter is apt to deride or devalue her mother during this time, for similar reasons. The same applies, except in this case it means to avoid the temptation to *support* her in these attempts. Above all, remember their focus on rules. Your job is to obey the rules, particularly as they apply to your status as ex-husband and father. Don't get caught cheating or fudging on these rules—these kids know what's right and what's wrong.

Finally, allow someone else to be important to your child. A teacher, a coach, etc. This doesn't threaten you, and it will be good for them.

7–10 Years
Your Child's Development

During this time children begin to develop a life outside the home. They have friends, they belong to clubs, they participate in organized activities, and they are developing images of themselves as individuals in a larger social context. Home is the base for these very important activities. Your child is developing competencies in areas that don't directly involve the family—school, athletics, social activities. She begins to form a network of significant others, although emotional ties are still almost exclusively to the home and those in it. Children at this age have an exquisite sense of justice, and are very much attuned to anything that "isn't fair."

In many ways, this is the calm before the storm, because puberty, with all its difficulties, hasn't hit. Your child should be happy-go-lucky and carefree most of the time, because the scope of his awareness is still somewhat limited. But lots of things are still happening in preparation for the changes to come.

YOUR JOB

This is a difficult time for many fathers, particularly those who are not in the home full-time. Your child is beginning to have a life of his own, one that does not always involve you directly. Other people occupy an important part of his life, and you may or may not even know them.

During this time your job is to keep up with your youngster. You need to allow him the freedom and mobility that comes with this stage, while not losing touch with his life. Many fathers come to resent those other important people, and take their importance as a personal rejection. This is a terrible mistake. Take pride in your child's participation in outside activities. Help him to take pride in participation without encouraging overachievement. Go to every ball game, every recital, every play. Stay involved.

This stage also requires rethinking of "visitation." Willingly take a back seat to lessons and practices, even if they occur on "your time." Allow your child to attend a slumber party on "your night." Don't be selfish. Your kid is growing up, and these are things that would take place even if you weren't divorced. It's just harder if you are.

10–13 YEARS
YOUR CHILD'S DEVELOPMENT

These are the dreaded middle school years. It is the rare middle school that truly has a good reputation. This is not an accident. These are very difficult years, in which the primary task of the youngster is to begin to form some semblance of a truly individual identity.

Kids at this age are notoriously group-oriented. They form cliques, which are highly exclusionary in nature. Virtually every child at this age feels like a misfit. And their solution is to identify with a group—and to hope that this group accepts them. They will tell you that they "just want to be myself," while adopting the exact dress, style, haircut, and mannerisms of a group. They will despise members of the other groups—until they actually become a member of one of these other groups. Then members of the former group will be despised.

Typically youngsters in this stage will try on a number of different identities until they begin to find one that "fits." They are trying to break the strong attachments of childhood, which will frequently place them in conflict with their parents.

Your Job

These are tough times for parents. To the extent that you can, you should be in close communication with your ex, both to offer support and to make sure you both know what your child is up to.

At this point you really need to begin to get to know your child's friends, even though he probably will resist this. Don't resent providing transportation to and from activities. By doing this you not only get to see your kid interact with others, you also get to know these kids and their parents. This will become increasingly important.

Your main task is to begin to be able to separate real trouble from simple posturing. Kids at this age don't have much judgment and they do stupid things as a matter of course. You need to be able to identify what things constitute "stupid things," and which are danger signs.

It is also important to remain a parental authority figure during this time, and avoid the temptation to try to be "cool" by being too intrusive. Give the kid room, but stay on top of things.

14–17 Years
Your Child's Development

Crunch time. Now your child is convinced that you know absolutely nothing. Puberty has struck, and adolescence is in full bloom. Your child will be full of insecurities and conflicts, but it is the rare adolescent who can admit this. Mostly, children at this stage find ways to avoid these conflicts—ways that tend to be obnoxious.

Conflict is the byword of this stage. They love you, but

they hate you. They need your support, but they don't know how to ask for it. They also don't know how to accept it. They have mixed feelings over just about everything. They don't want to go to church anymore. They want to drop out of scouts or other organized activities. Mostly they just want to hang out. More often than not you are simply an obstacle between your child and where he wants to be—which is usually with his friends.

Children in this stage want to be rid of parental authority, and any other authority, for that matter. Hormones are raging and they are frequently driven by forces that they don't understand. This is a very trying time for parents, but it is equally trying for the adolescent. We dare you to find *anyone* who claims to have had a great adolescence.

Your Job

This is a particularly difficult time for noncustodial fathers. You are not around full-time to see that this is really normal. Don't take it personally. Your child is in the process of becoming a young adult, and it's not pretty.

In many ways, your job is to let go, to let your child become a real person. Tolerate the weirdness and inconsistencies. Mourn the loss of the child you had hoped he would become (i.e., the better version of you), and allow his personhood to unfold.

Driving becomes an issue, with related safety concerns. Dating issues arise, with all the attendant sexual issues. Be prepared to deal with these from the standpoint of a *father*, not that of a peer. Remember that these issues may be more difficult for your

GUIDELINES FOR DEALING WITH
YOUR CHILD'S THERAPIST
BY J. RONALD HELLER, M.D., CHILD PSYCHIATRIST

Do
- ask to be involved in your child's treatment.
- be open and honest with me.
- ask me questions about the nature of treatment, costs, prognosis, etc.
- respect the confidentiality of the therapy.
- pay for services on time.
- bring your youngster to therapy on "your time."
- support your youngster's attempts to work through things.

Don't
- try to defeat or undermine the therapy; it'll only hurt your child.
- interrogate your child or otherwise intrude on the therapy.
- consult other mental health professionals without my knowledge.
- complain to your child about me, the therapy, the cost, etc. (Complain to me.)
- place your child in a position of having to defend me, the therapy, treatments, etc.
- use the therapy to propel *your* interests in a custody dispute.
- badmouth your child's mother, grandparents, stepdad, or anyone else to me.

child because of the divorce. Issues of drinking and drugs also come to the fore.

Don't let up. Continue to parent your child despite the difficulties. Temper your authority with trust and understanding. There is still a lot of water left to flow over the dam. Don't jeopardize your future relationship with your child. It doesn't do any good for *both* of you to be out of control. Stick to your guns, and support your ex.

17-PLUS

Usually, by 17 much of the storm of adolescence has passed. By this time many youngsters have part-time jobs and in many ways are handling their lives in a responsible manner.

At this stage your child should be looking toward separating from the home environs, either by continuing with school or by entering the work force and living independently.

Typically, group identity has given way to an individualized identity. Issues related to sexuality have matured to a great extent, and many youngsters have had at least one long-term relationship by this time. Many authority issues have also been resolved, particularly if the youngster has had opportunities to exert authority in his own right, either in a job, in organizations, or on the ball field. They are typically well on their way to becoming young adults, and depend on their parents primarily for advice, financial support, and guidance.

YOUR JOB

During this stage many fathers essentially become "partners" with their children, facilitating movement toward young adulthood. The child who had excluded you from his life and who was embarrassed by your very existence suddenly wants to introduce you to his friends. He tells them things about you that are flattering. He invites you into various aspects of his life.

God willing, your job at this point becomes a pleasure. You are in a position to help your child move into a semi-adult status, and your help will be appreciated.

Your dignified handling of the divorce and subsequent issues will pay dividends now, as your child has a greater understanding of you and your life situation, and shows a new respect and admiration for you. Now you begin to see that it didn't really matter who was "right." The job is done, and you can enjoy the fruits of your labors.

4

WHAT DIVORCE DOES TO CHILDREN
Becoming Aware

Must children of divorce always carry scars? Will they need enough therapy to employ a small army of psychological professionals? Are they necessarily on their way to being in the legion of the "walking wounded"? No! We believe "it ain't over 'til the fat lady sings." The first innings of your child's life might have been a little rocky. You also might have felt like you were "knocked out of the box." But the star of the later innings is the only one the fans remember. You can be that hero, the one who helps bring victory when there could have been a sound defeat. You can, with knowledge and caring, destroy the myth that divorce must lead to harm.

It has been well documented that divorce is bad for kids. You've read it in the paper, you've seen it on television, and now you've more than likely seen it in your own home. Dysfunctional marriages are not good for kids, either—make no mistake about it. But it is the rare child indeed who can truly say that he or she is glad that the parents divorced. Even kids who describe the most miserable situations you can think of, when push comes to shove, will still confess that they would have preferred that their parents stayed married. For better or worse, we tend to give up hope a lot sooner than they do. Or we don't have as much faith in ourselves as they have in us.

No matter what the particular circumstances, there are certain situations specific to the divorced child's situation that can be toxic and that can poison the child's development. These are issues we see in just about every child whose parents divorce. They can be dangerous if they are not addressed well. We are going to outline the most important of these and provide you with the "antidote" appropriate to each of these "poisons."

(((

POISON: DISRUPTING THE CHILD'S SENSE OF SECURITY

Kids can't imagine what divorce is like. Even though they can say the word and anticipate divorce, they have no frame of reference. Inevitably, an immediate response to divorce is a disruption in the feeling of security, the end of that sense that "God's in His heaven and all's right with the world."

Imagine. You're a kid, and you're going along thinking everything is okay. You've heard the word "divorce," but this is something that happens to other kids. Your parents may argue, and at times you may even worry about the "D" word. But you don't believe it. And then your mom calls you into the living room and says those four dreaded words: "We have to talk." And your heart sinks. You're scared. And you know immediately, on some deep gut level, that your life is about to change forever.

Antidote: Consistency and Predictability

You must accept that your child's sense of security has been disrupted. That trust has been broken. And maybe his heart, too. You can't wish it away. You can't pretend that "everything's okay." It will be hard, but this is something you'll just have to tolerate for a while. You also can't "talk" it away. Promises don't mean much right now. Your child thought he had a promise of two parents, and look what happened. Control your urges to "talk him out of it," because it won't work. Apologize, sure. Empathize. But don't expect this to restore his sense of security.

Security comes from close attention to detail *over time*. You have to *do* what you say you're going to do *when* you say you're going to do it. Down to the most minute detail. If you're going to go to his game, you'd better be at his game. Don't say you will just to please him. Better to have him hurt because you can't come than make a promise you can't keep.

(((

Poison: A Profound Sense of Loss

You'd be surprised how many folks come into our offices claiming that their children handled the divorce in "super" or "very mature" ways, and in fact show no ill effects. Sure, they say, the kids are depressed, but this is because of other things in their lives, not because of the divorce.

Wrong.

No child can go through a divorce without experiencing a profound sense of loss. No matter how pleasant the divorce seems, no matter how much "better off" everyone is since the divorce, your child will experience a sense of loss. As mentioned, he experiences loss of security. Loss of the marriage. Loss of the part of his identity that sees himself in an intact family. Loss of family outings, vacations, times spent together. The very real loss of a full-time father in the home. And there are other, more subtle losses that tend to be specific to each individual child that we can't even begin to generalize about.

Antidote: Let Him Find a Real Father

Again, first you have to accept and tolerate the fact that your child has these feelings. And that these are *normal* feelings under the circumstances. And that you have either caused or substantially contributed to these feelings. Manage your guilt. Control your urge to "make everything okay." There is no quick fix. Just as you have to mourn, so does your child.

Alleviate your child's sense of loss by letting him find the real you. Let your child find a father who is no longer burdened by the dysfunction in the marriage. A father who is not under stress or preoccupied with stress or a source of stress. A father who is a willing, enthusiastic, happy parent free to be a real father to him.

Again, this takes place over time. Don't rush things, and don't become impatient if it takes a while for your child to come around. It will happen.

(((

Poison: Reunion Fantasies

Children of divorce almost universally yearn for the parents to get back together. An intense wish for reunion remains, even if children not directly aware of it. The fantasy is that this will restore the sense of security and relieve the pain of the loss. Restore the intact family.

Even under the best of circumstances, these fantasies are active. They persist in children no matter how ugly or dysfunctional life was before the divorce. They frequently persist even after one or even *both* parents remarry! Sounds crazy, but it's true.

Some children will even go to great lengths to attempt to get their parents back together. They may feign illness to activate parental concern. They may act up at school so that the parents have to go to meet with the principal together. They may do an endless variety of things in an attempt to fulfill these fantasies.

Antidote: Build a New Reality Based on Fact

Again, you must remember that these fantasies are normal. Even though the notion of a reunion may be repugnant or utterly absurd to you, you're not the kid. Given what he's experienced, it may be very appealing to him.

You must remember that he viewed the marriage from his own perspective. With two parents, one home, and a sense that everything was okay. In spite of the conflicts, he had many moments of happiness and good memories.

Don't hold this against him. Be gentle with these fantasies.

Tolerate them. Address them gently but firmly with the facts about your new life, and your ex's new life. Whatever you do, don't encourage these reunion fantasies. You'll only break his heart. Address them gently and factually, with understanding and empathy.

(((

Poison: Guilt

Children view their world from a very ego- or self-centered perspective. They often relate things to themselves that in fact have nothing at all to do with them. They view themselves as having influence and power where clearly none exists. This is a normal part of kid logic, which often involves them making the most outrageous connections between events. It's part of their charm. But it also gets them into trouble sometimes.

Children also have funny ways of dealing with things they cannot control. They can't control much of anything, so they often pretend to control *everything*. This helps them feel more powerful in a world where things happen to them that are completely beyond their control. It stands to reason, then, that your child may see himself as responsible somehow for the divorce. Maybe if he had just behaved better, this wouldn't have happened. Maybe if he hadn't talked back or been such a bother. Essentially, maybe if he had just been a *better kid*, this never would have happened.

Antidote: Let Your Actions Do the Talking

We cannot state this enough. When you deal with adults, it's reasonable to think that your words can sway their thinking and get them to adopt a new point of view. Not so with children. And particularly with children whose sense of security and basic trust has been injured.

Reassure your child that he is not responsible for the divorce. Do it in a way that he can understand. Don't overdo it out of your own guilt. One clear statement is enough. If you say it over and over and over, he'll wonder why you're making such a big deal out of it. Show him through your actions that he bears no guilt, and therefore deserves no punishment.

Respect his mother. Keep your emotions under control. Handle your business appropriately. Help him control the things he *can* control, while showing him that he can entrust the things he *can't* control to you and his mother.

(((

Poison: Loyalty Conflicts

He doesn't stop loving his mom just because you did. And he doesn't stop loving you just because your ex did. He loves you both. He did not experience his mother in the way that you did, and he did not experience you in the way his mother did.

But he knows how you feel about each other. If he has fun with you, he feels like he may be letting his mom down. If he begins to feel himself getting attached to you, he may feel that he's betraying his mom. When he's not with you he misses you, but is afraid to tell his mom.

These conflicting emotions and perceptions intensify his guilt and place him in a very difficult position. He is torn. He may feel that he has two separate lives that can no longer be connected. He may feel that he has to watch what he says. He may have to constantly remind himself who he's with so he can know how to behave. He's always on guard, always a little anxious, uneasy.

ANTIDOTE: KEEP HIM OUT OF IT

Don't contribute to the conflicts by placing him in the middle. This is the worst thing that could happen to him.

Clearly affirm that your child loves his mother. Support her image in his eyes. Don't allow him to berate mom to gain points with you. Don't encourage his acting out against her. Don't let him disrespect her because he thinks you want to hear this.

When difficulties do arise between you and your ex, keep your child out of it—even if it involves him. Resolve your differences and present a united front. Don't *ever* disrespect her in his presence. Don't badmouth her, and avoid *all* sarcasm. He'll be afraid you'll treat him the same way someday if he makes you mad. Don't use him as the rope in a tug-of-war. Relieve him of this terrible burden, and let him just be a kid.

(((

POISON: SHAME

It doesn't matter that divorce is quickly becoming the norm. In many ways, it still represents a failure. It's something he will have to explain to others, even if he doesn't understand it himself. In the normal course of conversation people will make references to his "parents" that he may have to correct. He may not be able to spend the night with a friend because of visitation. Other kids may ask him why they never see his mom and dad together at games or at school plays.

These things weren't part of the original bargain; they aren't things he's been prepared for. He will have to adjust, and he will. But it makes him self-conscious. It makes him have to anticipate and deal with things that were not part of his experience before. No kid likes to have to explain such things, and no kid likes to feel conspicuous.

ANTIDOTE: PRIDE

Give your child a father to be proud of. Become a real part of his life. Help him to find areas of competence and encourage them. Find things the two of you can become competent at together. This can be anything. A stamp collection, a flower bed, singing. Anything! Teach him through your own actions that he can be proud of himself and of you.

Work through your feelings about his mom, so that you can go to games, plays, or any other activity where she may be. And when you do go, don't act like she's not there. Can you imagine how weird this would be for a kid? To see his mom and dad in the same room pretending the other is not there?

Keep him in mind. Modify your behavior to adjust to *his* needs, rather than expecting him to always have to adjust to yours. In other words: Be a man.

(((

POISON: PARENTAL PREOCCUPATION

You have not been in a position to throw yourself into parenting this child for some time. He hasn't been getting your full attention. Given what we know about his ego-centered nature, he may come to the conclusion that it's because he's simply not worth the investment. He probably hasn't seen you happy in a while. Again, he may believe that this has something to do with him.

He has not always seen you at your best. You have either been under stress or the source of stress. In any event, he hasn't gotten your best, your unfettered attention.

ANTIDOTE: LOOK HIM IN THE EYE AND TALK TO HIM
Sit across from one another. Talk. Play games. Learn some of the same things. Interact like real people. Avoid the mall. Don't let him get lost in TV or video games. Call your girlfriend *after* he goes to sleep. Treasure your time with him. Remove everything else from your mind for the brief time you are together. There will be plenty of time for the other things.

(((

POISON: A TOXIC ENVIRONMENT
He's been living amid conflict and stress for some time. This is an opportunity to provide an environment for him that is free from these things. He has likely seen you when you were not at your best, either as a father or as a person. Now is the time to correct this.

ANTIDOTE: POSITIVE, HEALTHY ENERGY
Provide discipline without temper. Let him see you engaged in positive relationships with others. By all means, get rid of all

sarcasm. It's destructive and ugly, and kids often don't have the sophistication to understand it. It doesn't hurt to laugh, either.

(((

POISON: GROWING UP TOO FAST

Think back to the arguments he's heard or seen. Was there an affair in the marriage, or a suspected affair? Was alcohol central to marital problems? Or sexual issues? Many times children of divorce have to come to grips with things they would not ordinarily deal with until later, when they would be better prepared. Normally, as children enter adolescence, a process of demystification takes place, where they cease to see their parents as ideal and godlike, and begin to gradually see them as three-dimensional, with strengths as well as failings. Divorce hastens this process, often before the child is ready.

ANTIDOTE: MAINTAIN THE BOUNDARIES

Once again, let him be a kid. Don't let your own issues influence you to allow him to be anything else. Not the "little man of the house," not your "pal," and not your confidante. He's a kid, and your job is to help him be one. Set firm, consistent limits. Respond to his questions in ways he can comprehend and process. Don't be manipulative. Be dependable, and allow him to depend on you. Don't force him to take on things over his head. He won't be a kid for long, and he probably has some catching up to do. Allow for some immaturity, but meet challenges with firm limits.

These are the most commonly seen "poisons" that can place your child at risk. While there are certainly others that we neglected to mention, and that may be present in your particular situation, these are the ones we see most in our offices. We hope that if and when they show up in your life and that of your child, you'll be able to see them for what they are and respond accordingly.

5

DEALING WITH DISCIPLINE
Becoming Respected

If we add up the number of years the authors of this book have been child psychologists, it comes to over 50 years. In fact, it's not unusual for us to find we were in practice before the parents of the children we're seeing were born. This means that the youngsters we've seen earlier in our work now appear in the Sunday papers. Where? They appear as brides and grooms. What does this have to do with discipline? Well, your child's future spouse is ultimately the one who will benefit from your not allowing your child to become spoiled. She'll enjoy a spouse who does not feel that the universe revolves around him. On your child's wedding day, his or her spouse really should thank you for having taken the time and effort to help him or her gain the ability to control themselves. Believe it or not, standing a boy in the corner will someday help make him a good husband.

If you want to see an otherwise sane and rational man turn into an absolute raving lunatic, just have him deal with a noncompliant child. A child who doesn't do what he's told. For some reason, this makes some guys absolutely nuts. Women (typically, but of course not always) seem to have far fewer difficulties in this area, blessed as they are with more patience, compassion, and understanding than we males. They may be prone to other problems, but they are less likely to absolutely lose it like men do.

Maybe it's "just our nature." Maybe it's the testosterone. Maybe it's *our* dads. Maybe it's a lot of things. The bottom line, though, is that men tend to place a pretty high value on compliance in a child. The noncompliant child isn't simply failing to do what you want him to do. This kid is also making a statement about your competence as a father. As an authority figure. And, in some cases, as a man.

Now seriously. Do you really want to give that kind of power to a kid who's lucky to get his Power Ranger underpants on right side out? Of course not. But believe us, it happens.

The problem is that too often discipline is seen in the context of *power*. One person (very powerful indeed) imposing his will on another (who has no power at all). When the one who has no power challenges the one who has it, sparks can fly. Grown men can throw tantrums of their own, and no one benefits, least of all the child.

All of the foregoing applies to normal situations. On top of that, the disciplinary tactics of the divorced father are always under scrutiny. There are those, most notably your ex and her attorney, who might like to view you as a sadistic monster. And the judge probably isn't too sure about you, either. He's heard lots of unflattering things about you.

The scenario is all too familiar: If you're not sadistic, then you're simply incompetent. Your child is a "monster" after he's been with you. His mother can't do a thing with him when he returns. It takes her until the next visit to finally straighten him out and get things back to normal—only to send him back to you to have you ruin him all over again. Clearly, a man in this position must be very careful in disciplining his child.

But kids *need* discipline. The last thing your kid needs is a father who is too frightened to discipline him. Or too guilty. Or too angry at the mother. Kids need to be taught when their behavior is unacceptable. It gives them structure and lets them know where they stand. When you draw the line, they know how far they can push. Not that they won't try to push more, and test you. But they know where the boundaries are. Believe it or not, this gives them comfort.

In fact, many of the problems we have these days stem from an absence of discipline. And not just problems with behavior, either. Obviously, kids who receive no discipline or inadequate discipline will behave in problematic ways. But there's an emotional and psychological cost as well. In our practices we often see kids who have inadequate discipline, and you know what? They're terrified. Scared to death. They would never admit it, but it's true.

Put yourself in the child's shoes. You don't know your rear end from a hole in the ground. And people can't discipline you. No one can control you. All of these people with all of their supposed power, and they can't control you. Then how on earth are you going to be able to control yourself? If no one can stop you, then what must you be capable of? If you're a kid and you believe no one can stop you, you're in big trouble. Because you are a kid, you have no judgment. You will keep going until *somebody* gets you under control. And often by then it's too late. You've already done irreparable harm.

Maybe it's not that they can't do it, maybe they're not *willing* to limit you. They don't want the aggravation, and don't want to expend the time and energy it takes to discipline you. You may have a lot of freedom, but underneath it all, you know. You know you need limits, and that the people who love you and are supposed to care for you don't want to go to the trouble. You're not worth it. This is depressing—doubly so, because rather than admit their failure, they'll blame you for your difficulties.

THIS IS NOT GOING TO BE EASY

So, you *must* discipline your child. Well. And consistently. You have a lot of things going against you. The popular culture does not do much to support parental control. Many of our institutions don't exert adequate controls over youngsters in their care. People sue other people for having the audacity to try to limit their youngsters, and too often they back off. Schools and other institutions struggle to administer discipline under these circumstances.

Life is tough out there, and more than ever kids need their parents to be resolute, firm, and steadfast. And here you are, divorced, with shared custody or no custody at all, and limited time with your kids. And you're likely co-parenting with a woman who is at best lukewarm about you, and who at worst is waiting for you to screw up so she can call her attorney and haul you back to court for being inadequate, undermining—whatever.

Did we say this is going to be tough?

We want to help give you the basics to build on to discipline your child with confidence and clarity. In spite of the fact that this will be taking place under a microscope. In spite of the fact that your ex may have a completely different approach in her home. And in spite of the fact that there are others who might like to see you fail. You can overcome these obstacles. You must. Because it's too important.

DISCIPLINE IS NOT JUST ABOUT COMPLIANCE

Controlling your youngster is certainly a component of effective discipline, make no mistake about it. But discipline is much, much more than that. The ultimate goal of discipline is to take a child who has little in the way of internal controls and to help build these controls throughout the child's development. It's no accident that it takes upwards of 18 years to socialize these guys. They come into the world completely unsocialized, or they wouldn't need us at all. There are a lot of complex, subtle, and at times confusing rules that they must master in order to adequately control themselves and fully participate in the culture. Discipline is essential in that process. It is central to your child's healthy development. It supports your attachment to your child. It's crucial to a solid relationship with your youngster. Consequently, it's absolutely central to your sense of yourself as a competent father.

WHAT IS DISCIPLINE?

Discipline is not simply meting out punishment. Discipline is an ongoing process. You can punish your child consistently every time he or she does something wrong. And you will likely have a compliant child. But this is not discipline, this is simply consistent punishment. True discipline involves much more.

It may be true that your child is more difficult to manage when he returns to his mother after being with you. These are difficult transitions, and none of us makes shifts like that with absolute ease. It may be that the rule structures of the two homes radically differ. It may be that he is attached to both of you and his loyalty conflicts make him anxious and difficult to manage. It may be that he hates to miss you when he's away from you, even though he loves his mother. The reasons may not have anything at all to do with the way you manage your child's behavior. But the ways you address his behavior can well *add* to the disruptions caused by these transitions if you're not careful. Therefore, changes in the way you manage your child can also help make these transitions easier for him.

Our message about discipline is like the rest of our messages. Don't be passive. Learn and learn and learn. Every bookstore and library has books on child-rearing and discipline. Even if you've never been a great student, this is a topic you should study; it's too close to your heart to be passed over lightly. There are lectures, discussion groups, and support groups dealing with these issues. Seldom does a semester go by that the local PTO doesn't offer a presentation on discipline. Churches will frequently present workshops or visiting lecturers who specialize in child-rearing issues. You have to study and learn.

If you're like many men, your only experience with discipline is what you experienced from your own parents. Don't fall into the trap of "Well, my old man whipped me, and I turned out okay." First of all, we're not sure you turned out all that great. Second, your dad's situation was very different from yours. Times were different, too. Don't try to do the same things your parents did in exactly the same ways. And for goodness sake don't try to do the exact *opposite* of what they did. Learn from their mistakes—don't let their mistakes dominate your parenting.

Learn, study, reflect, and formulate a disciplinary plan compatible with your philosophy of life, one that reflects your values and priorities. With any luck, you and his mother can agree on the major points of discipline and provide consistency between the two homes. If this is not possible, you simply have to do the best you can from your end. As we have noted previously, you can't control her, and the best thing you can do for your child is to simply do the best job you can. We want to help you help your child become a fully functioning member of society, and your handling of his discipline will be a key to this goal.

10 PRINCIPLES OF EFFECTIVE DISCIPLINE

1. COMPLIANCE IS NOT THE END-GAME

Compliance is not the only goal of discipline, although it is important. And punishment does not necessarily equal discipline. You can demand compliance and punish constantly, and you may well have a compliant child. But don't think that this means you're engaged in discipline. It is obviously very nice and gratifying to have well-behaved children. It makes us feel good and competent. But the true meaning of discipline goes much further than our own need system. It involves helping your child exercise self-control and trust his own internal controls. Making you feel good about your parenting skills is simply a positive byproduct of solid discipline. The real goal is to provide your child with the internal controls that give her self-esteem and the competence to become fully engaged in her environment.

2. UNDERSTAND DEVELOPMENTAL LEVELS

Some understanding of child development and developmental expectations is essential to effective discipline. You expect a two-year-old to throw temper tantrums when frustrated, and you simply "ride them out." This is a different story when the child is seven, however. By age seven he should have the internal control to deal with minor frustrations and delay gratifications. Tantrums at this age are inappropriate attempts at control and extortion, and thus should be met with discipline. You must be sure that the behavior you are disciplining is in fact inappropriate and under the child's control.

3. BELIEVE IT OR NOT,
SOME OF THIS STUFF IS NORMAL

Don't take this stuff personally. It's normal for children to resist; it's their nature. It's normal for them to want more control than they can handle, and to attempt to steal this control from you. It's normal for them to be rude, insensitive, selfish, and even mean. That's why we have to work so hard to make them as decent, sensitive, and lovable as we are.

Don't attribute adult motives to your child's behaviors. Your child does not have the breadth of experience to have these motives. Remember what it was like to be a kid. We know, we know, you *never* spoke to your old man the way this kid speaks to you. He would have clobbered you, right? Wrong. Odds are you *did* speak to him in that way, maybe more than once. And through discipline at some point you learned not to make that mistake again.

By the same token, don't hold a grudge against your child. You're the adult here, remember. Kids typically are just trying the best they can to get their needs met. Their methods are primitive and often annoying. But we're the adults and our teaching function is paramount. You can't teach if you're holding a grudge.

4. CLEARLY OUTLINE THE "DO'S," THE "DON'TS," AND THE "DON'T EVEN THINK ABOUT IT'S"

Kids need consistency and clarity. If your child doesn't know why she's being disciplined, you're in trouble from the start. Children need limits and boundaries. They need to know where they stand. Make sure your child understands the rules and the consequences for breaking the rules. Don't be afraid to be specific, and don't worry that your rules may be different from her mother's.

Having to adapt to the rules of two households is hard. That's just another reason that divorce is bad for kids. But it must be done. They have different rules at school, at the recreation center, and many other places. Don't hesitate to be very clear and specific about what's acceptable and what's not. Post rules on the refrigerator or on a posterboard in the family room. If the rules are different from the rules at Mom's house, so be it. You need to do what you think is best. Your kid will thank you for it someday.

5. Pick the Mountains You're Willing to Die On

Many rules are negotiable, and it doesn't hurt to have your child's input into the rule structure of the household. It's okay to compromise. Sometimes it doesn't even hurt to let the kid win, if the argument is solid and the situation's appropriate. We would not presume to tell you what values you should endorse. That is for you to decide in the context of your family.

But some things are far too important to be negotiable. Lying, stealing, and aggression against others are not acceptable under any circumstances, and must be dealt with swiftly and forcefully. Other behaviors are less critical, and will reflect your personal philosophy and, unfortunately, your own neuroses. You can make a clean bedroom the cornerstone of your disciplinary strategy if you want to. Or hair length. Or a pierced ear. Or any of a number of things. Our job is not to dictate what should be important to you. Our job is to encourage you to take an honest look at what you expect from your child, what things are critically important to you, and most importantly, *why* they are critically important to you. Once you understand what is important and why, you will be in a much better position to administer effective, healthy discipline to your child.

6. Don't Get Into a Stinking Contest With a Skunk

If you find yourself in a power struggle, and you are determined to defeat this little monster, but you don't know why, you're in

CHEAP CLICHES WORTH REMEMBERING

Catch your child being "good."

Never use your last resort first.

Deal with the behavior, not the person.

Never make a promise you can't keep or a threat you won't enforce.

Never try to control your child when you can't control yourself.

Never use your child's behavior to attack her mother.

The quality of mercy is not strained.

Some things are too important to be taken seriously.

Everybody wants to get to heaven, but nobody wants to die.

Just because you did it when you were a kid doesn't make it okay.

Never play poker with a man named after a city.

When you find yourself in a hole, stop digging.

If he doesn't know why he's being punished, you're in trouble.

Rule of thumb for time-out: one minute per year of age.

Kids have to rebel against something.

The first one is for the kid; every one thereafter is for you.

Never hold a grudge against your kid—you're the adult here.

Never forget the teaching function of discipline.

He will still love you tomorrow.

You don't need to compete with your ex for your kid's affection.

Your kid will have lots of friends—but only one dad.

You're in this for the long haul—keep your eyes on the prize.

Foolish consistency is the hobgoblin of little minds.

You're a competent, active co-parent, not an "absent father."

trouble. Always remember that you are playing from a strong hand. Your kid is attached to you and loves you. Whether you feel like it or not, you *are* the powerful one in the situation. You also have the benefit of experience and, we hope, some maturity and wisdom in the ways of the world. When the central focus of discipline deteriorates to the point of who wins and who loses, the whole deal becomes corrupted.

Try to anticipate issues that may become problematic and lay groundwork for dealing with them before they occur. You know from your own experience what your kid is apt to do or to get into. Don't get caught off guard. Have a plan. Anticipate the difficulties that may arise. Anticipate the way your ex may deal with them. And be clear and confident about your own position.

Kids don't have good judgment. That's why we need to exercise the amount of control that we do. If you get into a power struggle, your kid may go too far to prove a point, even to the extent of self-injurious or self-destructive behaviors. This is particularly the case with older children and adolescents, as they can take these struggles outside the home.

7. THE MOMENT YOU FIND YOURSELF IN A HOLE, STOP DIGGING

Wherever possible, avoid getting into a battle unless you're certain that you can win. Often, in the heat of the moment, parents will make silly pronouncements or make a threat that they cannot possibly enforce, and the child knows it.

Don't be afraid to take a break and reassess the situation. A "time-out" not only allows you to collect your thoughts, but it also models a very appropriate response to conflict for your child. Many youngsters are very adept at pushing your buttons, triggering your emotions and rattling you. You cannot control your child when you are out of control. Collect yourself. Remove the emotion from the situation. Model appropriate self-control for your child, and then come back and deal with the situation.

8. THE NATURE OF CONTINGENCIES

Only love is unconditional. Everything else has a price. We would all like for our children to listen to the better angels of their nature and behave simply because it's the right thing to do. Or because it will make us happy and proud and feel like good parents. Unfortunately, the better angels of their nature do not always prevail. That's why we have contingencies. Think about it. Most of us drive generally within the speed limit not because we're good people. We drive within the speed limit to avoid a painful consequence. We have a voluntary tax system, but we don't necessarily pay our taxes simply because we know it's the right thing to do. We do these things because the cost of not doing them is too great.

Contingencies are conditions we place on behavior: either rewards or punishments. Some parents prefer a system based on rewards, while others are more oriented to punishments. Obviously, the best system is one that incorporates aspects of both reward and punishment. How you reward or punish your child is your business. These are important issues, but we cannot dictate what you should do.

We can tell you, though, that whatever the contingencies,

they should be *efficient, meaningful,* and *close to the behavior.*

By efficient, we mean that the contingency can be delivered with ease. We've seen lots of reward and punishment charts and programs. They look good, but can be way too complicated and overwhelming. Which means they won't work. You need contingencies you can deliver with efficiency.

Clearly, contingencies must also be meaningful. If your kid doesn't yet understand the value of money, what good will it do to withhold his allowance? No matter what the contingency is, it should mean enough to the child to motivate future behavior.

Finally, you need to be able to deliver the contingency as close to the behavior as possible. Telling an eight-year-old that he won't be able to go to a ball game next month doesn't really have much impact, because a month may as well be a year to an eight-year-old. However, telling him there will be no TV tomorrow after school because he didn't observe his bedtime tonight is close enough to the behavior to be meaningful.

9. ACCEPT THAT YOUR CHILD'S JOB IS TO SABOTAGE YOUR DISCIPLINARY STRATEGY

This is what kids do for a living. They will try to exert their autonomy and their independence by defeating your rule structure. The older they get, the better they are at this and the more driven they are to do it. They will test you. They will push you to the limit. They will go to great lengths and show great creativity and ingenuity in their attempts to defeat you. It's their nature. They will rebel. They will prey upon your guilt. They will pit you against their mother, and you will come up short. They will probably also do the same to her, sooner or later.

So how do you respond? Do you give up because it's just too much trouble? Do you give in because you don't want to spend your time with them embroiled in conflict? Do you let them get away with things you know aren't good for them because you want to be the "good guy"?

Well, of course not. You do what you do in every other situation. You learn, think, and plan. You anticipate the ways that your child will attempt to defeat your disciplinary structure, and you have a back-up plan. And a back-up plan for the back-up plan. Don't get caught flatfooted. Don't assume that just because you said No, they will take No for an answer. You may be good, but we doubt you're that good. Be confident that your child will not respect anyone who cannot or, more importantly, *will not*, limit him. He already has friends; what he needs is a dad. Forget about competing with your ex for his affection. Forget about your guilt over not having been there at important times. You're here now, and he needs limits and firm, consistent discipline. Again, he'll thank you for it. Not now, for sure. But later, he will. We promise.

10. KEEP YOUR EYES ON THE PRIZE

Before you finish this book you're going to get real sick of hearing us say this. But it is clutch. It is your saving grace. You're in this for the long haul. Today will pass, and even if you obsess and wallow in it, your child won't. He has too much other stuff to do, like grow up. Take one day at a time. We have yet to see the singular act of discipline that forever ruined a child. And we have yet to see the one act of disobedience that forever doomed a child. Expect them to misbehave. Expect them to be angry and resentful when they have to account for their misbehavior. And expect them to try and outsmart you. Don't take stuff personally. Don't hold a grudge.

Keep your eyes on the prize, yes. But that doesn't mean falling into the trap of worrying about ten years from now. It takes you away from the here and now. Try to live in the moment. Guide your child. Love your child. Be a positive, proactive parent to your child. Model the self-discipline and control that you keep lecturing him about. Then enjoy him, take a deep breath, cross your fingers, and hope for the best.

NOT THE REAL QUIZ*
*(FOR THE REAL QUIZ, SEE PAGE 119.)

10 THINGS GUYS DON'T ALWAYS THINK ABOUT

1. How many times per week do you *really* change your underwear?
2. What percentage of the time do you *really* wash your hands after using the bathroom?
3. If you do happen to wash your hands, do you dry them with:
   (a) the nice towel provided, or
   (b) your pants legs?
4. When your mother sent you to brush your teeth, how often did you simply wet the toothbrush rather than actually brush your teeth?
5. Same scenario. How often did you just run the water in the bathroom and claim to have actually washed your hands?
6. What is the typical "shelf-age" of articles to be found in your refrigerator at any given time?
7. What color does bread have to turn before you discard it?
8. In your entire lifetime, how many rolls of toilet paper have you actually changed? (Just getting them out of the linen closet doesn't count, you actually have to put it *on* the roller.)
9. Do you have any idea which side the fork goes on?
10. Given the choice, would you *really* prefer to urinate inside?

DISCLAIMER (I.E., NOD TO POLITICAL CORRECTNESS): *Well, we did warn you that we would include off-the-cuff advice. But, seriously, we are aware of the dangers of stereotyping. We also know that the wisdom of emphasizing differences between the sexes is questionable. Maybe these generalizations don't apply to you. Our experience, however, tells us otherwise.*

Imagine that you and ten of your friends took this quiz. Consider what the answers might look like. Now, imagine if your ex and ten of her friends took this same quiz. How do you think their results would stack up against yours? Are you beginning to see why people may have some doubts about your ability to "single-parent" your child?

Obviously, the above quiz is a joke. But there are a number of things that women tend to think about intuitively that just about completely escape the male brain: issues of safety, hygiene, cleanliness, nutrition, and appearance. If you are ignorant of these issues in your own life, you may still manage to do okay. But you have the responsibility of raising a child, and such things are an important part of parenting. They make the child feel secure and taken care of. You need to remain aware of these things not only because your child will benefit, but also because you are operating under a microscope in many ways. People like your ex, and perhaps her attorney, are going to be very alert to the little "things that guys don't always think about."

BONUS LECTURE:
HOW YOU CAN LEARN FROM YOUR EX

Let's face it, there were a lot of areas where she might have been right. Whether it's genetic, social, cultural, or whatever, there are areas where women in general tend to be more attentive and skilled than men. They can spot dirt in places that men would never even think to look. They can *feel* clothing and tell if it's clean or not. Without even having to smell under the arms. This is not to say that all men are slobs, or that all women are not. But there do seem to be areas that men attend to less than women, and our job is to help you become more aware of these things. The long-suffering Mrs. McClure asserts that she can always tell which kid at the bus stop is staying with the father. He's the one in the T-shirt in 45° weather. Or she's the one wearing a plaid top and plaid shorts—and the plaids are different. Or they're the kid having a Snickers bar and a cup of coffee for breakfast.

Your job is to learn from your ex and to use her as a model. This is also the time to examine your own behavior. If you think she was a "clean freak" who couldn't stand the least little speck of dust, could it be that she was overcompensating for your sloppiness? If she was "overprotective" and a "safety nut," was this because you largely ignored safety or health concerns? For your part, did you encourage risky behavior to counter her overprotectiveness? Did you become lazy about issues related to health and hygiene because of her vigilance? Did you turn these issues over to her, or view them as simply "woman's work"?

If you are parenting on your own, you need to make sure you attend to these very important issues. Even if you're remarried, these are issues that *you* need to take responsibility for. Don't ignore them or turn them over to someone else. We have seen too many fathers who seem to wear ignorance of these issues as a badge of honor. Rest assured, you can attend to these most important areas and still keep your masculinity intact. These skills are the bedrock of parenting.

6

PARENTING AS A RELATIONSHIP
Becoming Responsive

*Your ex-wife might well have accused you of being unrespon-
sive and not interested in participating in the family. Maybe
she was right, but this is a new beginning.*

*The key to becoming a responsive parent is to clear your
schedule and your mind of everything except your child. This
is something most parents do not ever really achieve.*

*Years ago, the circus understood the principle. There might
be three rings, but when the star appeared there was only the
center ring—the only part of the big tent that was lit. Your
child is the main event, the top of the bill, the one you have
come to see. Have you paid for a ticket to the Big Top? Absolutely. You have spent thousands to be able to spend time with
your child, to say nothing of your emotional investment. Now
sit back and fully enjoy that which you have given so much to
see. This is a V.I.P. performance. At this moment, you are the
only ticket holder.*

*You have no task more pleasurable or more important than
being with your child. You have no wife who needs your time.*

Your workday is finished—now your major job is to keep all intrusions out. Your challenge—and for some parents it is exactly that—is to learn how to enjoy your child.

A NEW BEGINNING

This is the time for you to become a truly *responsive* parent—unburdened by the conflict, stress, and turmoil of a bad marriage or an ugly divorce, or both. No one could be truly responsive with such things going on.

But now you're in a much better position. By this point you should no longer be burdened by these things and should be free to attend to your child. To be responsive to her communications, verbal and otherwise. Responsive to the goings-on in *her* life. Responsive to her interests. To her hopes and dreams.

This is indeed a new beginning. An opportunity for you to parent, but also to do some things you may have missed yourself as a kid. You now have a built-in excuse to do "kid" things. This is one of the joys of fatherhood. Maybe as an adult you'd feel silly going to the zoo, or playing miniature golf, or going on an "explore" looking for nothing in particular. Perhaps your adult mind would tell you that you have no time for such frivolity. But these are things you can introduce to your child with a clear conscience. These things are part of fatherhood.

A wrecked marriage and a bad divorce may have caused the "kid" part of you to wither. They may have made it hard to laugh. They may have strained your relationships to the extent that you've become guarded and defensive. They may have prevented your child from seeing the kid in you. Well, here's your chance to wake up that kid. You're lucky, because this happens to be something that dads are good at. If you're a dad, they're part of the job description. Take advantage of them—you'll regret it if you don't.

THE MEANING OF "RESPONSIVE"

Certain questions always get a "yes" answer. If you don't believe us, just ask each of your friends if they think they're a good driver. *Nobody* will admit to being a lousy driver. But we know this can't be true, because we can't seem to get away from bad drivers. We curse them, we yell at them, and we may even introduce them to our own brand of "digital" communication. But, apparently, nobody actually is one of those people.

It's the same way with being responsive. Not many people will admit to being nonresponsive. Yet we know full well they're out there. In our practices we deal every day with their children.

Now's the time for you to take a good look at your responsiveness, apart from any accusations you may have heard during your marriage and divorce. If you truly haven't been responsive, now is your time to actively engage your child. If you feel your ex wouldn't allow you to be responsive, now's your chance to take charge on your own terms. If conflict and hostility squelched your ability to be responsive, now you're free. If you don't know *how* to be responsive, now is the time to learn. If you find, in your heart of hearts, that you really don't *want* to be responsive, you probably ought to get yourself into therapy, or "counseling," if you find that term easier to accept.

Being responsive to your child is not as difficult as you might think. When you drive your car, you unconsciously monitor engine sounds, the feel of the wheel, and your vehicle's overall behavior on the road. Even if you're thinking, talking to someone, or listening to the radio, at a very basic level you're monitoring the status of your car and responding to the feedback it's giving you. It's the same way with your child.

Many men make the mistake of thinking that they alone bear the burden of the relationship. These guys tend to force things. They set their own agenda of the way they think things "ought to be" (usually wrong), and forge ahead. Unfortunately, they don't attend to cues from the child, and they come off as controlling and domineering.

Other guys make the mistake of passivity. They think that their role is simply to react to the child and "follow the child's lead" in the relationship. They don't realize that they have a responsibility in directing and guiding their interactions with the child. These guys also do not attend to the child's cues, and they come off as distant and disinterested, like a dufus.

As in most things, the true course lies somewhere between the extremes. Being responsive is not a specific set of actions. It's a state of mind—of consciousness. Driving your car, you can have the mechanics of driving down pat, but if you're unresponsive to your vehicle and your surroundings, you run the risk of either an accident or a mechanical breakdown. When you feel the wheel shimmy at 45, you go to the shop and have your front end aligned. When you hear the sound of metal on metal every time you step on the brake, you have your brakes looked at. When you see someone ahead of you hit the brakes, you intuitively take your foot off the gas and begin to slow down. This is being responsive.

Sensitivity to cues and to feedback is essential. But sensitivity is meaningless unless coupled with a proactive response to these signals. So we want you to look at both sides of dealing with your child. First we want you to develop your sensitivity to your child's signals. Second, we want you to expand your repertoire of responding to this information.

THE ART OF "BEING" WITH YOUR CHILD

Before you can truly behave in responsive ways, you need to develop the responsive state of mind. It has several requirements. The first is to reawaken the child within you and resurrect it from the emotional wreckage of the divorce. This will give you the empathy and understanding needed to achieve the all-important next step: to see your child as a living, breathing, three-dimensional person in his or her own right, with *child* motivations, desires, attitudes, and dreams uniquely her or his own.

REAWAKENING YOUR OWN CHILD

Sometimes in the hubbub of daily life and with all of the responsibilities of adulthood, we lose touch with what it was like to be a kid. This happens to all of us, so you can only imagine what happens with divorce. You add financial problems, hostility, conflict, and a chronic and overwhelming sense of dread to the usual mix, and the kid within you may well wither and die. If this happens, you don't have a prayer of being responsive to your child.

With the divorce behind you, this is a good time to resurrect the child within you. Now, before you get all excited, this is *not* an invitation for you to be immature and irresponsible. It is also *not* an invitation for those touchy-feely new age things that require a guru.

No, when we talk about reawakening the child within you, all we mean—but we mean nothing less—is bringing back your *experience* of being a child, and integrating this with your present experience. You spent a long time being a kid, and most of what made you what you are today happened then.

But something weird happens around 24 or 25 years of age. We suddenly become adults, and we forget all of that childhood stuff. Believe us, it's true. How else can you explain *any* grown-up saying to a kid, *"I guess if Johnny jumped off a bridge . . . ."* Come on. Any adult who has truly integrated their childhood into their adult experience would never say such a thing to a kid.

10 Things Your Kid Will Quote To His Therapist Someday If You're Not Careful

"Don't be a baby"

"If your friends jumped off a bridge, I guess you would too"

"You can't have your cake and eat it too"

"You'd cut off your nose just to spite your face"

"You're just like your (fill in the blank) . . . ."

"Can't you do anything right?"

"I'll give you something to cry about"

"You'd lose your head if it wasn't attached"

"Stupid is as stupid does"

"You got that from your mother's side of the family"

You can only understand yourself in the context of your own development. Without this, you won't understand your kid.

You will misinterpret her motives, treating them too much like those of an adult. You won't understand natural developmental things, which will make you critical, uncaring, or mean. Most important of all, you'll miss the richness and magic of your child's experience, because you've forgotten your own.

If you're in danger of forgetting, then do whatever helps you recapture your childhood experience. Listen to or read people like Bill Cosby or Garrison Keillor, two men who have retained an exquisite sense of the wonder and weirdness of childhood. Go back to old photo albums. Think about your third grade classmates and the things you used to do. Remember how important "stupid" things were to you at various points in your development. Remember how quickly things changed, how the plain girl down the street all of a sudden became a goddess to you. Remember how important "fitting in" was, and how you felt that your parents never understood. Remember how great it felt to be liked, to be noticed, or to finally find something you were good at.

Even if your childhood wasn't pleasant or even if it was damaging in some ways, you need to do this. Surely there were some great moments of happiness, excitement, and wonder in spite of the traumas. Maybe you'll discover something about how resilient kids are by examining your own painful experiences. This will be especially reassuring and instructive if your own kids have been through the wringer.

They Love You . . . It's Their Nature

It's important to understand certain universal things about children. For instance, how forgiving they are. With the possible exception of dogs, children are the most forgiving beings on the planet. They are constitutionally incapable of holding a grudge (thank goodness). Adults carry grudges; children have to be taught. Even when they've been injured, it's their nature to want to forgive and move on. So, if you feel guilty over some of the things you've said or done, don't let this interfere with your relationship. Odds are the kid has already forgiven you and is just waiting for you to forgive yourself.

Even though you may be able to carry a grudge (even against yourself), they won't. They'll forgive. And forget. They don't have any investment in staying angry with you or staying hurt. Unlike your ex, it doesn't benefit them in the least to keep you in a position of feeling guilty or down on yourself. To the contrary, they have a huge investment in seeing you become free, happy, and available. They benefit from having you in a position of being emotionally "there" for them and attending to them, not "owing" them out of guilt or being "one down" in the relationship. That's the stuff of bad marriages, not of good parenting.

Kids are genetically predisposed to think you're the greatest—no matter what you may think of yourself. Believe it or not, it would take more than what you've done to destroy this. Even youngsters who have been seriously mistreated continue to wish for a good relationship. Your kid needs you and wants a relationship with you, even if you've been a jerk.

Your kid doesn't care about what you've achieved, how much money you make, or how big a house you live in. He doesn't care about how guilty you feel or how angry you are at his mother. He cares about how available you are to him. He cares about how much of your time he can share. He cares about how much of your life you will let him into. He cares tremendously about what you think of him. And it means the world to him *that* you think of him.

Kids come into the world totally dependent. They depend on you for their physical safety, for their sense of security, and for their overall sense of well-being. Think about it. They *need* to see you as competent, under control, and, above all, caring. Don't deprive them of this.

They also often see the real you, even when you may not. They can sense your sensitivity, your moods, and your strength. Even if you can't. When you're with your kids, you must see yourself through *their* eyes. They like you. They admire you. Believe it or not, they would give just about anything to be like you (frightening thought, huh?). You don't need to prove anything to them. You simply need to relax and let them love you.

Don't be defensive—it'll make you look like a jerk. Don't try to impress them—they're already impressed. Don't be passive—they'll feel lost. Don't try too hard—it will make them uncomfortable. Don't assume that they see you the way their mother does—they don't. And, above all, don't be fake—they can spot fake from the other side of the globe.

Be yourself. Be confident, be strong, be relaxed, and seize every moment to simply "be" with them. Even if your children are young, you don't have much time. There will come a time when this will all change. When they become teenagers, they will need to see you in a very different light. They will need to challenge you. They will need distance from you. They may even need to defeat you. That's why it's important to forge a solid relationship now. The kind of relationship you can establish with them during the early years will, to a great extent, determine how well both of you can weather the storms of adolescence.

What Do Dads Do?

If you had a particularly unsatisfying marriage, you may have forgotten what dads actually do. If your ex defined your role rather than letting you develop your own "dadness," you may have a distorted notion of what dads do. Part of reawakening your child is to remember your own dad. For example, do you remember:

- that one game of catch with your dad was better than a hundred games of catch with friends?
- the feeling when he'd let you steer the car (even if he kept his hands on the wheel the whole time)?
- how much fun you had when your mom would visit her sister out of town and leave you with your dad?
- how good it felt when he'd let you sleep in his T-shirts?
- being amazed at how big his hands were when he crossed the street with you?
- how cool it was when he'd slip you a little money or candy when mom wasn't looking?
- how safe it felt knowing he wouldn't be scared of the things that you were scared of?
- that even if he didn't smell so good sometimes, things just seemed to be better when he was around?

Earlier we mentioned some things your ex seems to be able to do just by second nature, things that you perhaps never think about. Well, there's also a lot that you have to offer these kids that perhaps she never thought about.

Your kid may see you as uniquely identified with a whole range of special things—things like:

throwing a knuckle ball, making his initials in a really cool way, calling her "Princess," whistling through your teeth, wiggling your ears, building Indian village projects, belching, breaking in a new fielder's mitt, learning to hit with the label of the bat up, listening to bad music too loud, telling her her dress is pretty, calling him from work just to say "hi," the wonders of Vienna sausages, taking a fish off the hook, dancing silly to bad music, teaching her how to have a sense of humor, coming into his room when he's had a nightmare, bringing presents home from trips, the wonders of poker, tying cool knots, driving, making him feel loved.

And hundreds more. This is the time. If you've been through a hideous divorce, you have already been robbed of some of these things, and of precious time. Now is the time to get with it. Appreciate your child's experience, and start responding with your own unique "dadness."

COMMUNICATION

> FATHER: "So, how are you doing?"
> SON: "Okay."
> FATHER: "How was school today?"
> SON: "Alright, I guess . . ."

FATHER: "Anything new?"

SON: "Not really."

FATHER: "Any homework?"

SON: "A little, I guess."

FATHER: "Anything you want to talk about?"

SON: [Shrug]

Sound familiar? We hope not. But this very conversation will take place today all across the country. In many households it has become a ritual. The parent feels obligated to ask these "important" questions, and the kid likewise feels obligated to provide the minimum required response.

Of course, this conversation will take place in many homes where the parents are still married. But we're more concerned about *your* home—and conversations between you and *your* child.

Also be assured that the burden is not on your child to be more forthcoming. The burden is on *you* to be more responsive.

Let us tell you about a couple of kids we've had the privilege to know, and how they experienced their dad's responsiveness, or lack thereof.

A 15-year-old boy recounted an incident that happened on his "visitation" with his dad. The assault of puberty had caused him to become discouraged about his appearance, and he questioned not only his acceptability, but also issues related to his sexuality. He was embarrassed to discuss these issues with his mother, and looked forward to getting some help from his dad. They were busy all day Saturday with dad and friends, and dad went out on a social engagement (read: DATE) Saturday night.

Tennis was scheduled for Sunday morning. At several points he dropped hints to his dad that he wanted to take a rest, but without success. Noon was nearing, and he needed to be returned home by one. Finally, he missed a shot and simply picked up the ball and walked around the net and asked his dad to talk. The response he got was: "We're not here to talk, we're here to play tennis!" They finished their set and went home. So, instead of talking to his dad, he talked to one of us.

Another boy, in very similar circumstances, had the opposite complaint. ALL his dad wanted to do was to "talk." He didn't want to play catch, he didn't want to drive golf balls, he didn't want to play anything. He wanted to TALK! The kid felt the talking was more like interrogation. It was unnatural and artificial, and it was clearly more for the father's benefit than for his. And he hated it. He liked and admired his dad, and wanted nothing more than to just "hang" and relate to his dad. He wanted to meet his dad's friends, be a part of dad's life. But his dad felt the need to "talk." So the kid increasingly began to schedule outside events on "Dad's time" in order to avoid this discomfort. And he got more and more depressed.

If either of these dads were responsive, they would know when to play and when to talk. They would know how to mix the two. They would be guided by the child's tempo. They would be less concerned about their own agenda.

ATTEND TO THE TEMPO

As adults, we tend to be governed by schedules, clocks, and deadlines. We have to adapt ourselves to external factors beyond our control. And *because* we're adults, we are equipped with the flexibility, awareness, and maturity to conform to this state of affairs.

Even if you "don't feel like talking," when the boss says "Let's talk a minute," you talk. Even if you don't feel like it, when your turn comes up in a meeting, you talk. When you have other things on your mind and your current love interest says, "Can we talk?" you put these things aside (we hope) and talk. Even if you "don't feel like it."

Kids aren't equipped this way. Kids have a tempo all their own. They don't always come through on demand. Sure, sometimes it's resistance. But not always. Mostly, it's developmental. If you want to guarantee that all you get is a shrug, a mumble, or a "whatever," just try to make your kid talk to you on *your* terms.

Think back. Try to remember what it was like to have to sit across from an adult, *any* adult, and simply talk. On their terms. About anything, much less about your feelings. What did you do in these situations? If you're like most of us, you clammed up, shrugged, mumbled, and simply endured it until you were dismissed. Usually by a frustrated and perhaps even angry adult.

THE GREATEST CONVERSATIONS

Talk to your friends. Ask any father you know. They'll all tell you. The most amazing conversations take place at the weirdest times. Stopped at a red light on the drive to school. Supervising bath time. While you're shaving or getting dressed for work. While you're cooking dinner. Or most often, when you're trying to read the paper, catching up on your work, or engaging in some other activity that's important to you. Because kids respond to their own tempo, not to yours. They don't make appointments to talk. They are never "ready to talk." They talk when the spirit moves them. It's part of their charm. They don't pull this stuff up on command. It just hits them at the moment and they let it out.

That's why you'd better be there when that moment comes. Not just being there sharing the same air, but really BEING there. Being responsive to him when he's dawdling around your desk aimlessly, just sort of hanging around and being a pain. Being responsive to her when you think the conversation is over, but she doesn't leave. Being responsive when his questions seem silly, or even annoying. Responsive when she's "just trying to get some attention." Because these may be cues, clumsy attempts at getting you involved or keeping you engaged. Because there's something on your kid's mind.

When you were overwhelmed with misery or exhausted from the stress of your marriage (or divorce), you may well have missed these cues. You can't afford to let that happen now. Now is the time to clear your mind and pay attention. To be watchful, and let the scene unfold. If you can do this, you may well be touched beyond your wildest dreams. For these are the times that your child will open up the windows to her soul, and you'll be amazed what goes on in there. But you'll see it only for a moment, because then it's gone.

Your conversations with your child are too important to be all routine. There will be times when you need to suspend your attention to everything else and focus only on the moment. Don't just listen with your ears. Listen with your head, with your complete free-floating attention, and most of all, with your heart. Children can't always communicate what they really mean. The words they use may be inadequate. Your job is to *experience* the communication coming from your child—what he says, how he says it, and also what he *doesn't* say. Your child needs for you to respond to the emotional content *behind* the communication, not so much the specific content.

Don't jump to conclusions. That happens when you're attending to *your* agenda. If you don't understand, relax and go through it again. Let him know that you are asking questions because you want to understand, and not because he's not making sense. Even if you don't understand, you owe it to him to at least try. If you do, he will *feel* like he's been heard, whether you understand him or not.

So be there. Don't be caught up in a day-to-day grind that robs you of these opportunities. Take the time to be responsive, even if it means putting down the paper or saving the document you were working on. These are the precious moments.

You Don't Always Have to Talk to Communicate

Children can relate to a quiet man. Don't feel pressured to be the life of the party. Much can be communicated during periods of silence. Sometimes it's okay for two people simply to be together, sharing the silence. Being responsive doesn't mean you have to carry the burden of conversation. Watch kids and learn. They can sit for long periods saying nothing, but they relish the companionship and shared experience.

You don't always have to talk to communicate. If you are relaxed and comfortable in your child's presence, she'll know. She will feel it, experience it. If you are anxious, impatient, or uncomfortable with periods of silence, she'll feel that, too. And she will soon begin to experience silence the same way, and then she'll avoid these moments. Don't ever feel forced to engage her in conversation. Relax, and enjoy being in the same room. Be available, be relaxed, and be open, and you'll *be* there. It means a lot.

THIS IS NOT A CALL TO ACTION

Rarely will your child bring issues to you because she wants you to solve them for her. If you've ever tried to give a child advice, surely you know this. The need to solve a problem and get it over with is part of *your* neurosis. Your adult mind is action-oriented and solution-focused. Not hers. She's talking to you about it because she simply needs to be heard. She needs a sounding board, to hear herself think out loud. She doesn't need a quick fix. If she did, she wouldn't be talking to you, she would have fixed it herself.

She may need to ask a question out loud in order to formulate an answer—so resist the temptation to offer a solution. Listen to what she says and ask questions that will help her explore whatever's on her mind.

Don't impose your feelings on her, and don't tell her how she *should* feel—she'll clam up. Rather than solving the problem, your job is to help her understand how she feels and why.

OFFER ALTERNATIVES

Whatever you do, don't expect them to do what you would do. It's the kiss of death. The ideal situation is one in which you can, through responsive probing and listening, lead them to a point where they will make a decision on their own. Not because it's what you would do or because you have told them to—but because you have helped them clarify their own feelings and develop a perspective on the issue. One way to do this is to present a range of options, some appropriate and some ill-advised and damaging. The last thing they want is to be told what to do. But if you can help them to reach a decision on their own, everybody wins. Be patient. Your experience allows you to see the big picture long before they can. Listen, empathize, and expand the range of possible options, and more often than not you will be rewarded.

This Isn't About You

You're grown up. You've been through this before. You handled things in your own ways, some good, some not so good. You no doubt are convinced that you have the right answers, even if you yourself did not employ them.

If your child wants to know about *your* issues, he'll ask. If he wants to know how *you* feel about peer pressure, hip styles, or any other aspect of his life, he'll ask. In that event, feel free to talk about your feelings and your ways of handling things, because that's what he's asking for.

But when he comes to you with things on his mind, he needs *your help, not your autobiography.* These discussions are not about how you would have handled the situation or how you would have felt. It's about your kid, who's in the midst of the situation right now. Resist the temptation to impose yourself on the situation and offer solutions that you would employ (or wished you had). Keep your own emotions out of it. Your child is confused enough as it is. If the conversation begins with his difficulties and ends with a discussion of you and how *you* would handle things, conversations like this one will become increasingly rare.

NORMALIZING YOUR LIFE IN AN ABNORMAL SITUATION

We humans are a funny lot. We're capable of tolerating incredible discomfort, stress, pathology, and trauma, and, just like the Energizer Bunny, keep on going. True, when the trauma is immediate and blunt, we'll shut down. This is seen in certain psychiatric conditions like battlefield "shell-shock" or what we now call post-traumatic stress disorder. These reactions are a clear sign that the system is overwhelmed and needs a break. In psychiatric jargon, these would be termed responses to "acute" stress or trauma.

However, when the trauma is less intense and occurs over a protracted period, we show a remarkable ability to adapt and carry on. These insidious, ongoing types of trauma are termed "chronic." While the death of a spouse might be termed an "acute trauma," divorce and protracted custody litigation fall into the "chronic" category. We are equipped with a wide range of defense mechanisms that allow us to tolerate chronic stress and still function. And thank goodness for that. Otherwise, we all would be completely immobilized at one or more points in our life. During times of substantial stress and trauma these defenses can be your best friend. They protect you and allow you to go on. They give you distance from the emotional intensity of the situation, insulating you from its full impact.

But these defenses can also be your worst enemy. In our practices it is not at all unusual to hear the complaint, "I didn't know just how deep a hole I had dug for myself until I got up and stuck my head out of it." Or, "I don't know how it went on so long. Now that I look back on it, every minute of it was pure hell." Looking back on these times, we are often amazed and bewildered at how we got through them.

Defenses can be *internal*, like the ones Freud wrote about—defenses like denial, rationalization, and others designed to distance you from the emotional impact of the situation. But defenses can also be *behavioral*.

Make no mistake about it, drinking more than one or two cocktails or beers on a regular basis is defensive in nature, because it's designed to numb and to help you escape. Working too much may be socially very acceptable, but it can also be a defense against having to face going home. Overinvolvement in your child's life can be a defense against guilt or against being seen by others as disinterested. In fact, doing *just about anything* too much or too often is likely to have strong defensive elements. These can serve a very important function during the times of stress and trauma. But they can also prevent you from recovering afterwards.

This is a pitfall for a lot of men going through a nasty divorce and custody battles. It's easy to become so accustomed to modes of defense that they continue well past the divorce and past the point of their usefulness. They become like old tennis shoes. They may have holes in them and they may smell terrible, but, doggone it, they're *comfortable*. And they're less of a hassle than going to the shoe store and trying on new ones and breaking them in. But there comes a time when we have to change our ways of adapting because our circumstances have changed.

Now that you're through the divorce, it's time for you to

change the way you do business. If you dealt with the stress of a doomed marriage by becoming a workaholic, now is the time to construct a leisure life for yourself. If you dealt with it by becoming so busy that the things you were running from couldn't possibly catch up with you, now is the time to stop and smell the roses. If you dealt with it through drinking or other "numbing" behaviors, now is the time to stop that stuff and start living. No matter how you managed to get through it, now is the time to reorganize yourself and set about normalizing your life.

Now is also the time to recognize how your child survived the stress and confusion of a good marriage gone bad. Just like you, his defenses may have protected him from the trauma, but now is the time to let them go and develop new ways. He'll need your help, and you can't help him unless you first straighten out your own affairs.

We've already discussed what divorce does to kids. They have endured a situation in which they had little control, and they no doubt developed their own ways of coping.

- Did they turn to friends and outside activities for security?
- Did they lose themselves in sports or some other activity?
- Did they withdraw into their own world?
- Did they become provocative and aggressive?
- Did they protect themselves by becoming too agreeable, too passive?
- Did they blame everyone else for their problems?
- Did they show their distrust by questioning everyone's motives?

- Did they start to hang with the wrong crowd?
- Did they *become* the wrong crowd?

No matter which courses of action your child took, you can help. First, you can help by normalizing your life—by getting healthy again, either mentally or physically. By getting in control again. By restoring balance to your life. And, most importantly, by resuming your role as a parent. Now is the time to learn to plan again, to put energy into your surroundings, to get back into a routine, and to assert your role as a father.

THE REAL QUIZ

Here's another quiz for you, and this one's no joke. If you don't get a perfect score, get to work. And don't quit until you score 100%.

1. Do you know how to operate a child car seat and do you put your youngster in it *every time* you go out in the car? Even if it's just a quick run to the store?

2. Do you know what supplies your child needs for homework?

3. Do you have enough *appropriate* clothing to anticipate various changes in weather when your children are with you?

4. Do you have a cookbook in the house?

5. Do you know how to read food labels to determine what is healthy and what isn't?

6. Do you know that blue and green don't go together?

7. Do you have a home health encyclopedia?

8. Do you know when to brush off physical complaints and when to call the doctor?

9. Do you know how long different foods last in the refrigerator and in the pantry?

10. Do you understand the effects that disorganized, chaotic, or dirty physical surroundings can have on a child?

11. Do you know where your "girlie magazines" are? More to the point, are you *sure* your kids can't get to them?

12. Do you know how to wash, dry, and iron clothes? Which laundry detergents are best for kid's clothes? What goes in hot or cold water?

13. Do you know how to pack a healthy lunch for school?

14. Do you know which side your child's hair is parted on?

15. Is your house "kid-proof"?

16. Do you know when to give aspirin and when to use a non-aspirin pain reliever?

17. Do you have a home First Aid kit, with the Poison Control Center number on it?

18. Are you aware of the top ten most common accidents around the home and how to prevent them?

19. Do you know all of the telephone numbers you will
    need if something should happen?

20. Do you have any idea how much it means to a kid to
    have his father attend to these issues?

7

EARNING ACCESS TO YOUR CHILD'S WORLD
Becoming Involved

In reflecting on this chapter, a story came to mind from long ago in grammar school.

On a cold day a man was walking along a country road, happy to have his old coat to keep him warm and protect him from the elements. The sun and the wind were watching the man, and in sport decided to make a wager as to which could most quickly make him remove his coat from his shoulders. The wind went first and blew and blew. But the more fiercely it blew the more tightly the man pulled his jacket around him. Then the sun came out. The sun bathed the man in the warmth of its bright rays, and very soon the man took off his coat. But as soon as the sun went away and the wind resumed, back on would go the coat.

As old as this story is, it still applies to you. If you've been under marital tension and responded with bluster and rage like the wind, you can now act more like the sun and put your child in a better position to drop his self-protective coat. But, like the sun, you must maintain that warmth. Protective layers woven from the hurt of family strife take time and effort to remove.

Like the sun on cloudy days, a father must work to keep shining through. We have seen fathers do exactly that. When they do, they find that they are invited into their children's lives.

We've known fathers who have fought to the ends of the earth for the right to see their children and to influence their growth and development the way a father should. But, after they won, they didn't know what to do with their victory. They didn't know how to integrate their children's lives with their own, particularly when their time with their children was so limited and seemingly artificial. As a result, they spent time with their children, but, at times, their hard-won victory seemed hollow because their children's lives really revolved around their mother's household.

Things don't have to be this way. As we reviewed these cases, these fathers seemed to share one or more traits:

- Their divorce left them empty and without energy.
- They remained sad and resentful—even after they had "won" time with their kids.
- They let financial hardship keep them from finding ways to enjoy their kids.
- They just wanted "peace and quiet."
- They thought kid's stuff was just that—"kid's stuff"— somehow beneath them.

In other words, they just didn't get it.

If you find yourself identifying with these guys, now's the time to take a good look at yourself. Because, if you're still

124

wallowing in any of these traits, you won't have much to offer your kids.

THE WORLD OF THE CHILD

If you live alone, you perhaps spend Saturday mornings sleeping in, or running errands, or catching up on work, or going to the gym, or pursuing any of a number of "adult" activities. But do you know where your eight-year-old is? She's kicking butt with the Power Rangers (or whatever show eventually succeeds that one), saving the earth with *Captain Planet* (or its equivalent), or feeling superior to all those little dweebs who watch *Barney* . . . while she secretly enjoys it herself.

And where do you think your ten-year-old son spends his Saturday mornings? No, he's not doing homework. He's saving princesses, vaporizing ghouls, earning extra lives by eating "power pods" or something, and destroying the very enemies of civilization. Because he's playing video games.

And what about your teenager? While you're listening to NPR or the local country music station, she's listening to stuff you can probably barely imagine, let alone grasp.

If you truly want to relate to your children, you can't expect them to do the things you do. They're not built that way. No, your job is to learn as much as you can about *their* world, to find life where *they* live it. Not necessarily to join into this life, but to at least have familiarity with it and to be able to share parts of it with them. You need to find the places where your kid lives. Find how she spends her time. Find who he "lives" with in there. And find ways to gain entry.

If your kids are like most, there are certain doorways leading to the places where they live. We want to help you find the keys to these rooms in your child's life. And develop ways to keep these doors open.

If you don't, these rooms and their contents will become your enemy. They will compete with you for your child's time, and they'll win. They will provide ways for your kids to shut you out. And they'll make your kids strangers. Our goal is to help you to expand the areas of common interest and experience with your kids.

Door no. 1: Television, Video Games, The Web

For lack of a better term, we'll call Door #1 "Popular Culture." It's a tough door to open, because it involves doing things that you're most likely not interested in. But, like it or not, this is where your kids live a significant portion of their lives. It bonds them to other kids, it keeps them up on the newest trends, and it provides hours of mindless "entertainment" for them.

Keys

- Watch TV, even if it hurts. Get to know the heroes, villains, and other characters in their lives. Watch it *with* your kids. If you see stuff you don't like, ask them why they like it. Challenge them, if you want. Talk about it, discuss, it. You might learn something about your kid. But you can't do this if you're not familiar with the stuff. You'll have no credibility.
- Play computer or video games. Understand the concepts behind their fascination. See what your kids find so ir-

resistible. Know who the characters are, what the "secret codes" mean, and what the big attraction is. Play with your kids, but *don't compete*. First of all, no adult can beat a ten-year-old mind at this stuff, and, second, it will do your kid good to whip your butt at something. Again, though, you can't criticize it from a standpoint of ignorance. If you find something to be critical of, you need to be familiar with it first.

- Read the websites, magazines, fanzines, comic books, or whatever vehicle of popular culture your kid enjoys. It will be an eye-opener, for sure.
- Listen to the music. OK, maybe not *all* of the music. But some. Tune in to their radio stations for as long as you can stand it. Listen to the language that's familiar to them. Familiarize yourself with the themes that make up the music they enjoy. Again, if you don't agree with the themes, you're in a much better position to challenge them if you at least know what they're listening to.

On the Other Side
- You'll find what makes her laugh, and what makes her sad.
- You'll find out who his heroes and villains are, and why.
- You'll learn a little about the pressures they're under.
- You may find some things she's good at.
- You'll find a room in which you can share some space with her.

Door-Slammers
- Compete with him in video games and be a poor sport

- Tell her that . . .
    the styles she likes
    the music she likes
    the TV shows she likes
    her latest heartthrob
        . . . are all "stupid."
- Use your access to this room inappropriately, to . . .
    - be "one of the guys";
    - play the morality police;
    - provide adult criticism;
    - or to act like a jerk in any other way.

Door no. 2: School

Your kid spends a tremendous part of his life here. It's where he's expected to be competent, polite, social, studious, and capable. It's where he competes with other kids his age, kids you don't even know. He may complain about it profusely, but, apart from the home, this is where he spends the bulk of his life. And this is where he has a tremendous number of important, formative, experiences. But this is also an area that may be fraught with conflict. This may be an area that your ex has tried to shut you out of. So be careful.

Keys

- *Participate!*
- Join the parent/teacher organization.
- Go to parent conferences.
- Go to "Back to School Night"—and everything else.
- Get to know her teachers.

- Get to know the principal.
- Develop ways to find out about homework.
- Join your kid for lunch, if allowed and if possible.
- Arrange to receive progress reports and report cards.
- Chaperone dances, field trips, etc.

On the Other Side

- You'll learn how your kid responds to structure, authority, and the world at large.
- You'll get a glimpse of how others see her.
- You'll see how competent he is.
- You'll learn about other kids her age.
- You'll see what he's learning.
- You'll see what she's interested in.
- You'll see how he relates to others outside of the home.

Door-Slammers

Embarrass him by . . .

- acting like a jerk with his teacher or principal (being demanding, controlling, flirtatious—you know the routine);
- treating him like a kid when you see him at school;
- showing up at school with someone whose presence he'll have to explain;
- bad-mouthing his mom to these people;
- making him feel inadequate in any way;
- making him feel stupid;
- competing with him to prove how smart you are; or
- criticizing his work as "baby-fied," simple, etc.

Make her feel defensive by . . .

- criticizing the teacher
- badmouthing her peers
- talking about how things were so much better way back when; or
- making fun of anything about her school, classwork, or friends.

DOOR NO. 3: SPORTS AND ACTIVITIES

This is an exceptionally important room in your child's life. These activities give your child a chance to find out where he shines. Whether it's sports, music, art, or any other area where your child can develop her talents, it's of vital importance. This is especially true for kids who are not gifted students, for it provides other avenues for them to demonstrate their competencies.

KEYS

- *Get Involved.*
- Coach, but only if you have the disposition; if you don't, find other ways to help out. Volunteer for other jobs to support the cause.
- Attend every possible play, game, recital, concert, etc. Even if they're dreadfully boring. And even if it means that you'll be thrown in with your ex, her new man, old friends, or whatever. *Go!* You cannot underestimate what it means to your kid to have you there. Sometimes *because* they know how boring it is for you. Sometimes *especially* if these other folks are there. It just makes them feel good.

10 Ways to Break Your Kid's Heart

1. Promise to . . .

   Come to his game

   Go to her play

   Pick her up at a certain time

   Get him a particular gift

   . . . Or anything else

   . . . And then don't.

2. Spend your time with him either preoccupied or in a lousy mood.

3. Forget *any* special occasion (birthday, graduation, award ceremony, etc.).

4. Give away *anything* that belongs to her without asking—no matter how old or useless it seems to you.

5. Let him see you . . .

   In flagrante delecto

   Drunk

   Stoned

   . . . Or anything else that would make him ashamed of you.

6. Pay more attention to your girlfriend than to your daughter.

7. Pay more attention to your girlfriend's children than to your own (even if you *do* see them more).

8. Be selfish, self-centered, and more interested in your needs than in his.

9. Criticize, belittle, or make fun of the things she likes.

10. Badmouth his mother.

WEDNESDAY EVENINGS....

- Be a cheerleader! Support her, no matter whether she's good. Let him know you're rooting for him, even if he spends most of his time on the bench.
- Applaud effort, not results. You can't control the results. But you can encourage, support, and appreciate the effort. That's your job. Results are determined by lots of things that neither you nor she can control. But the *effort* is hers and hers alone. Encourage and applaud it.
- Make sure he gets to every practice, every rehearsal, and every team party, bake sale, etc. Even if they occur on what you mistakenly think is "your time."

ON THE OTHER SIDE

- You'll find how well he's learned the lessons of sportsmanship.
- You'll see her develop a sense of diligence in practice and in mastery of skills—a work ethic.
- You'll get a chance to see how well he's learned principles of teamwork.
- You'll see how she relates to other kids in an area completely unrelated to you.

DOOR-SLAMMERS

- Be a "stage father," "Little League father," or otherwise act like a jerk.
- Lose your temper or hold your kid to a different standard than the other kids.
- Lose control of your own issues over competition and sportsmanship.

- Refuse to let him attend functions because they impinge on "your time."
- Yell too loud, be profane, or otherwise embarrass him with your behavior. Better you should just stay home.
- Criticize the activity in any way. If your son shows talent in dance, support it. If your daughter can crush a softball over the leftfield fence, support it.
- Forget for even one minute that this is not about you. It's about your kid.

Door no. 4: Life with Friends

This is another room where your child spends much of his time. These people have a profound influence on your kids, and often in ways that you cannot be aware of, or control. And often your child's loyalties may become conflicted between you and the peer group. This is a very important room.

Keys

- Get to know your kid's friends. Know them by name. Know where they live. Don't be nosy or intrusive, but know who your child is spending his time with.
- Get to know their parents. Be in a position to call the home of a friend if necessary. This is your best defense when "everybody's doing it."
- Let her friends get to know you. Provide transportation when you can. Attend gatherings when you're invited. Let them get to know you for the man you are. They may have heard some ugly things about you, so you must be careful to just be who you are.

- Open your home to them. Have them over to your home as much as possible. Give them a safe, friendly place to "hang." Talk to them, and let them talk to you.

ON THE OTHER SIDE

- You'll see how your kid relates to other kids in noncompetitive settings.
- You'll overhear conversations that will make you laugh, some that will make you cry, and some that will make the tiny little hairs on your neck stand up.
- You'll learn which friends you can trust and which ones are weasels.
- You'll get a chance to see your son as he really is, in unguarded moments with his friends.
- Maybe you'll remember what it was like when you were a kid, with *your* friends.

DOOR-SLAMMERS

- Be intrusive, be nosy, try to stick your nose into places where it doesn't belong.
- Try to be "one of the guys," a "chum." You're not. You're a dad.
- Be overly judgmental of her friends.
- Be overly critical of the time he spends with his friends.
- Limit their time with friends because it's "your time" — it's not your time.

DOOR NO. 5: IN THEIR HEADS

This is a most precious room indeed. It contains her most pri-

vate thoughts, fantasies, wishes, and desires. It is a room that
is guarded closely at all times. A room that is filled with awe,
wonder, curiosity, and not a little fear and dread. As child psychologists, we can attest to what a carefully guarded room it is.
This is where we do our work, and we have trained for years
in techniques designed to gain access. It's not a room you can
just barge into. Entry is gained very slowly and in very small
installments.

KEYS

- Trust. First and foremost. Your daughter doesn't have full
access to this room herself, and she's not going to just let
anyone in at any time. She doesn't understand much of
what goes on in there herself, so she's vigilant about letting anyone in. Your son holds his most precious fantasies
in here, and sometimes they embarrass even him. He's not
going to let just anyone in.
- Your presence. We discussed this before. There's no substitute for *being there*. Because you don't know when that
door might just swing open. And if you're not there, you
missed it. It's gone. Maybe not forever, but you don't know
when it'll blow open again.
- Your attention. We've said this before, too, but some things
bear repeating. *Be there* when you're being there. Don't be
preoccupied. Be available, even if there's nothing going on.
- Your respect. This sounds trite, but we mean it. Respect
the contents of this room. They may seem silly to the adult
mind. They may sound egocentric and weird. And they
may sound angry and frightening. But you must respect

them. Their real, they're part of your child—who is part of you. Don't treat them lightly, or you'll never see them again.

On the Other Side

- You'll find the essence of childhood.
- You'll find a six-year-old who's been given the keys to the car—to unlock the doors—then sitting in the driver's seat and, in his mind, looking around to see all of these people who are absolutely amazed that he can actually drive a car. Imagine that! And at his age, too!
- You'll come upon a young girl looking in the mirror and fixing her hair. And you'll know that she knows exactly what it's like to be crowned Miss America. Because it's happened to her a thousand times.
- You'll see a nine-year-old boy bouncing a tennis ball off the front steps. And you and he will be the only two people on earth to know that in fact he's the world's greatest shortstop making an amazing play in the ninth to save a one-run lead.
- You'll see a girl who's quiet and withdrawn. Who's giving subtle signals that something's wrong. And you'll know instinctively that something's wrong, because you've been given a pass into the room.

Door-Slammers

- Forget what it was like when you were a kid.
- See the contents of this room as scary, silly, or worthless.
- Ridicule her when she shows you a glimpse of the room.

- Tell him to "grow up" or "stop living in a fantasy world."
- Blame your ex if you don't like what you see.
- Any of a million other things you could do if you were self-absorbed and insensitive.

Door no. 6: At Mom's House

Like it or not, this is where he spends the most time. This is where she will watch *most* of her TV, listen to *most* of her music, and play *most* of her video games. This is where he will have his friends over *most* of the time. This is where he will practice his music *most* of the time. This is where they'll do *most* of their homework, *most* of their studying, and *most* of their school projects.

And worse, this is where he'll be when the coach calls him to congratulate him for making the all-star team. This is where the school will call if there is a medical emergency. And this is where she'll be when her boyfriend calls to break her heart. And you won't be there. Like it or not, this is a most important room in your youngster's house. Don't shut yourself out.

Keys

- A healthy respect for your child's attachment to his mother—no matter how you feel about her.
- A healthy respect for the fact that this is what your daughter calls "home." This is where most of her life transpires.
- A genuine concern for, and interest in, his life in your ex's home.
- The strength to tolerate the fact that her life might be going quite well *in spite* of the fact that she's living with your ex

most of the time.

- Your ability to work through your feelings about his mother in ways that don't involve him.

On the Other Side

- A child who can negotiate the very daunting task of dividing his loyalties between two households.
- A child who can genuinely love her mother *and* her father, in spite of their differences with each other.
- A child who feels confident and comfortable with herself, because she knows she's loved by both of her parents.
- A child who is willing to open all of the doors because he sees that you can be trusted with his most important thoughts, fantasies, wishes, desires, and feelings.

Door-Slammers

- If we have to make a list of these, you're on the wrong page.

These are the doorways through which you may gain access to the life of your child. There are no magic combinations to the locks on these doors, no "golden keys." As always, common sense and a continuing focus on the best interests of your child will give you access to every single door. And your child will be there to welcome you into each and every room.

8

BRINGING YOUR CHILD INTO YOUR WORLD
Becoming Accessible

For some reason, not many men seem to focus much on bringing their children into their worlds. Maybe they think no one else cares about how they spend their time. Maybe they don't think their interests would interest their kids. Or maybe they're defensive, because others have criticized the ways they spend their time. If any of these descriptions fit you, we suggest, for the sake of your kids: Get over it!

Think of the things your kids may have heard about you.

"All he cares about is . . .

> golf
> football
> TV
> that damn car
> himself."

"He's a workaholic."

"He's lazy."

You can fill in the blanks, we're sure. The only way you can counter these claims, the only way you can show they're false, is to let your child into your world. With enthusiasm and joy.

Because you are a noncustodial father, the time your child spends in your home is naturally different from the rest of his life. But this does not mean that it has to be abnormal. It does mean that the responsibility is on you to make it as normal as possible—even if this means some sacrifice on your part, and even if you meet with resistance from your child. This effort will be critical in establishing the kind of relationship that will help your child grow.

So, let's examine the various rooms in *your* world, and see what keys might unlock them for your children, so that they can get to know the real you in every facet of your life.

Door no. 1: At Your Job

For better of worse, this is one of the larger rooms in your personal home. If you're like most, you spend a great deal of your time here. A great deal of your energy. And much of your thinking, worry, and preoccupation.

Most divorces occur when children are young—at a time when you're in the earlier stages of your career. When you felt you couldn't "slack off" without jeopardizing a promotion. Or when your job security was rather uncertain. So maybe your kids do have some feelings about your job. But whether they do or not, we know that they have some distorted notions about what you actually *do* at your job.

Remember what you thought your dad did all day? The authors know what *our* kids thought. Since we're psychologists, we can't discuss anything involving patients. So Saffer would talk to his kids about the interesting things he heard from people he had lunch with. And his kids grew up thinking he "had lunch" for a living. McClure's children, on the other hand, knew that he did a lot of testing. But their notions about testing came from school. So they thought he spent his time taking math tests, spelling tests, and so on. In short, they thought he was nuts. So let your kids see what you really do all day.

Keys

- Take your kids to work at every opportunity. Let them see what you do. Even if you don't think much of your job yourself, their only interest is in you. They want to know how you spend your time at this mysterious place.
- Introduce them to your colleagues. Let them get to know the people you talk about in your conversations. People who like you. People you have things in common with.
- Educate them about what you do. Even if you fear that it's boring. They want to know. Some of the stuff you do might even be cool.
- Make yourself available to them at work. Make sure that they can reach you when they need to. Make sure your colleagues will know who they are and put them in touch with you.

On the Other Side

- They'll find a side of you that they have never seen.
- They'll see your work ethic, and hopefully pattern their own after yours.
- They'll see you interact with others in a different way, in a way governed by different rules.
- They'll see that you are competent and respected by others.
- They'll begin to understand what you have to go through to get the money you provide for them.

Door-Slammers

- Devalue your work and what you do.
- Complain about work all the time in their presence.
- Model a poor work ethic for them.
- Fail to show them the joy in making a living and providing for your loved ones.

Door no. 2: Play

Odds are this was an area of conflict in your marriage, and it may persist as a sore spot even after the divorce. The ways that a man spends his leisure time are frequently a bone of contention in the marriage. Even in intact marriages. Spouses are often jealous of the time their husbands spend in leisure activities, particularly when those activities do not involve them. When husband and wife play golf together, the wife rarely complains about the time it takes. Time spent golfing with cronies, however, seems a lot longer. To make matters worse, as the marriage deteriorates, the husband often spends more and more time in these outside activities. This only increases their negative charge.

So, remember that your leisure time may be somewhat tainted by what your children may have heard. Approach it with some caution, and make sure that you keep things balanced.

Keys

- Listen carefully to the criticism. Try not to be defensive. She might have been right. If you really are obsessed with golf, football, swing dancing, or anything else, get some balance and moderation. This is first and foremost.
- Involve your kids. If you're into golf, bring them along. Even if they don't want to play, let them drive the cart. If they do play, be patient and go slowly.
- Let them see the attraction. Educate them. Don't force the issue if they aren't interested, but at least give them a flavor of what you find appealing about it.
- Develop other new interests more in line with things that they find appealing.

On the Other Side

- They'll see your joy, your enthusiasm, and your happiness.
- They'll get to see you at play, unfettered by the routine burdens of the rest of your life.
- They'll see healthy models of competition, sportsmanship, and pleasure.
- They'll see new areas of competence that you've developed.

Door-Slammers

- Prove that your ex was right when she said you were obsessed with your activity.
- Force your kids to try to learn skills they're not ready for or not interested in, and then belittle them when they resist.
- Place your leisure interests above your interest in spending quality time with your kids.
- Take it too seriously. Let it become more like work than play. Be miserable when things don't go the way you want. Make leisure time seem like work.

Door no. 3: Your Friends

These are the people who share the good times with you. People who provide you with support, and people who care about you. They are indeed a very important room in your house.

But this is also an area that may have been experienced by your child as fraught with conflict. Friends may well have competed for your time when you were married . . . and won. If so, your kids approach this area already somewhat jaded, and you must handle it with care.

Keys

- Let them get to know the people who bring you happiness. When you do things with your kids, invite friends along when appropriate.
- Take your kids to picnics, parties, and other activities where your friends gather.
- Encourage close friends to send them birthday cards, con-

gratulatory notes, etc., to your home, if they like.

- Let your kids know that these people are resources. Your child can depend on them, just as you have.

ON THE OTHER SIDE

- Very importantly, in the wake of divorce, your kids will see you in successful, positive social relationships.
- They'll meet other people who like you, and who value who you are and what you have to say.

DOOR-SLAMMERS

- Expose your kid to inappropriate behavior on the part of your friends.
- Place your friend's needs above your child's.
- Overdo it in any way.
- Let your friends badmouth your ex in front of your kid.

DOOR NO. 4: OPERATING YOUR HOME

Believe it or not, this is also an important aspect of your life. It says much more about you than you may be aware. Your kids are alert to how you manage your household, and they naturally compare it to the way your ex does what she does. Like it or not, it *does* say a lot about you.

KEYS

- Chores. Give your kids ownership in your home by giving them appropriate responsibilities within it.

- Model good behavior by performing your own chores happily in a timely manner.
- Develop a sense of routine, purpose, and pride within your home.
- Afford your child with clean, private, and personal space, and let her have input into how she manages her own space within your home.

ON THE OTHER SIDE

- They'll find a solid role model for
  - . . . pride in ownership;
  - . . . respect for property;
  - . . . order and responsibility;
    - . . . and lots of other good stuff.
- They'll find a dad who organizes his home for their benefit.
- They'll find a dad who is willing to share (perhaps contrary to what they've heard).
- They'll find a sense of ownership in your home.

DOOR-SLAMMERS

- Be a jerk. Make chores a burden.
- Go about your own responsibilities with a frown and reluctantly.
- Be a perfectionist.
- Be selfish and anal about your home.

Again, it really doesn't matter *what* the activity is, whether it's leisure-oriented, maintaining the home environs, or performing your job. What matters is your enthusiasm, your interest in sharing the activity with your kids, and your experience of joy when you are with your child. If this seems an alien concept to you, perhaps it's time to call the shrink.

9

MANAGING
THE VISITATION
Becoming Effective

Certain relationships have no names. What do you call the father of the man who's married to your daughter? What do you call the brother of your daughter-in-law? What do you call the man living with your ex-wife (careful!).

What do you call the period when your children are at your home? Is it a visit? No, they really live there part-time. Your children coming to your house isn't really visitation. How can they visit their own home? The fact is, this is so complicated there is no real name for it.

You also have a job that hasn't really been defined. What you've been presented with is the task of normalizing the unusual. You are also asked to combine the mundane (chores, homework, etc.) with the exciting (spending time with your kids).

We want you to know that "uncomplicating" the complicated is a skill you can perfect. You can then teach it to your children as well, which will put them in good stead for the rest of their lives.

Making Your Place "Kid Friendly"

Relocating your dwelling is way up there on the "Stress Index," which measures the stress caused by different events. Divorce is up around number two (just behind the death of a loved one), and moving is not too far behind. So you can imagine that moving under circumstances of divorce is an incredibly stressful and uncomfortable event. Even if there's a part of you that's kind of excited about setting up a new place of your own, it's still stressful.

You need to remember, though, that this is really *not* a "place of your own." It's a place where you will live *with your children*, even though your children will not be there full-time. This is an important point. It means you may have to suppress your desires for a "bachelor pad," replete with portable bar and disco ball. You may have to postpone your notions of "getting back to the land" and having a dwelling worthy of *The Waltons* or *Little House on the Prairie*. And you certainly must squelch your inclination to keep a home the way you did when you were in college, or like when you first moved out on your own. You need more than an empty spool of underground cable for a table and planks of wood on cinderblocks for shelves, to make a nice home. Sheets over the windows for curtains and human-sized, light-up bottles of Miller's High Life for wall treatments just won't make it. And NO, we repeat NO pictures of Pamela Anderson on the walls. Or anywhere else.

As we've said, one of our goals is to help normalize your child's life. When you were married there was never a question about making the home "kid friendly," with plenty of space for kids and plenty of stuff to do. *That priority has not changed.* Even though you're not married, you're not "single." You're divorced. Even if you feel like you're a bachelor again, you're not. You're an ex-husband. And a father. Not a bachelor. And you can't live like you are. When you put your new home together, you must do so with your children in mind.

Many of the suggestions we're about to offer may seem ridiculously self-evident. In fact, we hope so. But, you know those little packets of chemical crystals they pack stuff in that have a warning in bold type—**DO NOT EAT**? Well, why do you suppose they had to put that warning there? They probably had a very good reason, you know?

We wouldn't make this stuff up. We make these suggestions because we've encountered parents who have done some pretty crazy things. Besides, we did promise to make specific, down-to-earth suggestions.

---

10 KEYS TO A "KID FRIENDLY" HOME

YOUR "KID FRIENDLY" HOME IS:
1. CLEAN
2. WARM
3. COMFORTABLE
4. BRIGHT AND CHEERFUL
5. SAFE
6. ONE THAT AFFORDS PRIVACY
7. ENTERTAINING
8. FILLED WITH GOOD, HEALTHY FOOD
9. ACCESSIBLE TO OTHER CHILDREN
10. FULL OF YOUR KID'S STUFF

---

1. CLEAN

Even though your kids may be slobs, they appreciate a clean home. *Dirty* should be distinguished from *messy*. They can handle some mess and some clutter. But they can't handle filth, grime, and dirtiness. The incidence of asthma and other childhood ailments is striking these days, and a less than clean home will only make these things worse.

2. WARM

You'd be amazed how many kids complain to us that their dad's house is cold. Maybe their dads are hot-blooded. Maybe their fathers just don't get cold. Or maybe they're just cheap. But we do get these complaints. So make sure your kids are warm. Even if you happen to be very comfortable, have plenty of coverlets and warm stuff on hand for them.

3. COMFORTABLE

You don't have to have expensive furniture. But you *do* have to have furniture. And not just straight-back chairs and a deacon's bench, like one dad we know. Real, overstuffed furniture. Or beanbag stuff. Or great big huge pillows. Kids like the feeling they get from comfortable stuff, just as much as they like the feeling they get from being warm.

4. BRIGHT AND CHEERFUL

It's a home, not a mortuary. Pay attention to the colors on the walls and to the amount of lighting. There's plenty of research to suggest that people, and especially kids, are highly sensitive and responsive to their physical surroundings. Keep it colorful, bright, and cheerful.

5. SAFE

Do a safety check. (More about this later.) Make sure your home is structurally sound, with no exposed wires or obvious dangers. Check for fire hazards. If you have a yard, make sure there's no broken glass, sinkholes, rats, or loose pit bulls out there.

6. AFFORDS PRIVACY

It's okay for kids and step-kids to share rooms (same-sex, obviously). As long as they have privacy. Privacy in their room when they need it. Privacy in the bathroom and for dressing. And also privacy *from* you. You may think you look like Brad Pitt when you're undressing, but your kids don't need to share the moment.

7. ENTERTAINING

We're not suggesting you convert your home into the "media center." We don't even care if you have a TV. What we do care about is that there are plenty of fun, age-appropriate things to do. It's no good to simply tell your kids to go entertain themselves if there's nothing for them to do. You need books to read, games to play, areas for outside play, and activities to do.

Public libraries are a bountiful resource of cool things to do—probably the most underutilized resource in the nation. They constantly have children's programs and they offer a cornucopia of books, magazines, and other fun stuff. And it's all free. If you're in an urban area, check out the museums, and look for the children's programming that they offer. There are all kinds of resources out there for those with little free cash on hand, and they're easy to find. All you need is the desire and a little creativity.

In addition, sometimes kids *do* need to be entertained. They may need assistance to structure their activities, even in play. They may need assistance in developing ways to pass their time fruitfully. And they may need help in learning new things, new ways to spend their time. And maybe, just maybe, what they really need is for you to attend to them. Besides, that's what you should be doing, anyway.

8. LOTS OF GOOD, HEALTHY FOOD

Come on, surely you know that kids like to eat. And they don't always like Slim Jims, Vienna sausages, and other stuff that you might like. They need *kid* food. Healthy food, of course, but stuff they'll eat. And a fair amount of it, too. The last thing on earth you want is your kids going back to their mom complaining that there's nothing to eat at your house. Or telling their teachers. Or their grandmother, God forbid. Even if you don't cook, there are plenty of good, healthy things you can have on hand. A few supermarket chains even have a food consultant who can tell you the kinds of things you need to have on hand for children at different ages. Your child's pediatrician is a good resource, too. Many pediatric groups have staff nutritionists who'll be glad to help you. Ask.

9. ACCESSIBLE TO OTHER CHILDREN

Hopefully, your new home will be in a neighborhood of some

sort. Not in some "singles complex" or way out in the woods somewhere. There's no substitute for having other kids around. It's good and healthy for your kids to make friends and form attachments to kids in your neighborhood. You'll also get the opportunity to watch them in their play, which is priceless. You'll see parts of them you didn't know existed. It will also help them look forward even more to their time with you, if they know they'll be playing with their new friends.

10. FULL OF THEIR STUFF

If you're playing your cards right, not one square inch of your refrigerator is visible to the naked eye. Instead, it's covered with stick people, suns with smiley faces, and all manner of other strange and even questionable creations. Announcements from school. "Best Student of the Week" awards. And all kinds of other stuff. It would also be nice if your kids can't enter any room of your house without seeing pictures of themselves somewhere. Except maybe the bathroom, but in our opinion, this room is fair game, too. The house should be full of their clothes, toys, books, and belongings of all types.

We know you're not wealthy, and we know that this whole business has been a strain on your wallet. If you're like most, you're also now maintaining *two* dwellings, or at least you're contributing significantly to another dwelling over and above your own. But poverty is no excuse. Just keep your priorities straight, which means: Keep your kids at the top.

WHEN THEY'RE IN YOUR HOME, THEY'RE YOURS

We can't emphasize this enough. When your children are with you, you're in charge. It doesn't matter how their mom does things. It doesn't matter what kind of rules she has. You're in charge here. Obviously, a good degree of consistency between the two households would be desirable, and you are certainly free to follow your ex's lead in structuring your own household. But this is not mandatory.

If you're unsure of your own competence, don't solve this problem by depending on your ex to tell you what to do. Get competent! Don't solve the problem of lack of knowledge by relying on her to teach you how to do your job. Get knowledge! Don't use the excuse of not "being in touch with kid's stuff." Get "in touch"!

This is your home, these are your kids. If you run your household differently from your ex, then you're teaching your children to adapt to different situations. This is a valuable life skill. And they can adapt. Kids know that there are different rules for church, for the playground, for school, and for the shopping center. And they can also adapt to different rule structures between two homes.

But—and this is a major "but"—you also have to construct your home situation in ways that serve your child's interests. There are times when this may mean that you'll have to temper your own parenting philosophy to best meet the needs of your children.

For example, if their mother is adamantly opposed to kids having toy guns and other weapons, and you happen to belong to the NRA, you don't do your kids any favors by loading them up with these kinds of toys when they're with you. You're making things hard on them. If your ex has a psychotic break every time she hears the words Pokemon or Barney, you don't help your children any by encouraging their fascination with these creatures.

This is not "caving in." This is not designed to accommodate your ex or to cater to her whims. This is solely to preserve your child's sense of continuity between the two homes. Which is good for them.

Unfortunately, issues such as these can be a invitation to mischief. Just like with pick-up times, clothing, and the other logistics of visitation, these issues can present a great temptation to express hostility toward your ex. Many of her deeply held beliefs can be used to get back at her. You can do all kinds of things during your time with your kids to make her nuts. But this would be wrong. Most of all, it would be an extreme misuse of your time with your children.

You should also know that accommodating certain of the mother's wishes is not specific to the divorce relationship. This happens in all marriages and all partnerships. And it's tough, it takes its toll on even the best marriages.

Your job here is not to agree with your ex-wife's views, or even to give them much credence. Your job is to do what is in the best interests of your child. If you have differences with your ex, then address them *outside of your relationship to your kids.* If you address these issues and they cannot be reconciled, then you simply have to deal with it. This is a part of being divorced (and of being married, for that matter). Plus, as a noncustodial father, you don't exert enough control to always manage this situation in the way that you would like. You have to make the

...AND EVERY OTHER WEEKEND

best of it and manage it in a way that doesn't hurt your child. It's your job.

But, on a happier note, you really are in charge of them when they're in your home. The way you parent your children in your own home will reflect who you are. It will let them get to know you better than anything you could ever tell them about yourself. So believe in yourself and treat your children to the real you, the real you in your own home . . . their home. Be assertive and be competent. If there are issues that you're unsure of, get out there and learn about them. Structure your home in a way that fits your philosophy, your parenting style, and your notions about how you want to raise your children. And hope that you and your ex at least share these things in common.

KEEPING YOUR CHILDREN SAFE

First and foremost among all concerns during "visitation" is safety. Earlier we talked about things that just seem to come naturally to mothers and that often barely enter the consciousness of dads, and safety concerns tend to fall into this category.

Perhaps it's the need to be "macho." Perhaps it's to overcompensate for mom's perceived "overprotectiveness." Perhaps men just don't need to be as sensitive to danger as women, or perhaps they don't have to worry about it because the women do so much. Or perhaps men simply express their protective instincts differently than women. But you know what? All of these "perhaps" don't matter. What matters is providing the safest environment for your kids that you reasonably can.

We don't want to belabor the issue, so we'll just give you some helpful hints and specific recommendations.

SAFETY INSIDE THE HOME

We've already mentioned the structural aspects of your home and its environs. Now for the things inside.

TOXINS

These are among the leading cause of injury, sickness, and death to youngsters within the home.

- If you have younger children, purchase cabinet guards to keep them from opening kitchen cabinets, particularly the ones under the sink. That's where we keep the toxic, poisonous stuff, and they're right at "kid level."
- Keep all lawn and garden stuff (fertilizer, pesticide, etc.) well out of their reach and under lock and key, if possible. Kids love to explore, and they'll find it, trust us.
- Contact your local Poison Control Center. They will provide you with stickers you can place on anything toxic; teach your kids what they mean.
- The Poison Control Center will also provide you with emergency numbers and emergency first aid in case your child ingests toxins. Keep in the home and have readily accessible syrup of Ipecac, distilled water, ingestible/activated charcoal, and every other substance they recommend. But call them first. You need to know what to use for the specific toxin ingested.
- Most importantly, HAVE A PLAN. Know exactly what you're going to do in case of an emergency. Who to contact. Who can sit for the other kids when you go to the Emergency Room, etc.

FIRE

Fire is right up there, too, in terms of accidental death, injury, and harm within the home.

- Teach your kids fire safety. Check with your local fire station to see what educational materials they have for kids.
- Obviously, keep all matches, lighters, etc., well out of reach. Rather than making such items so taboo that they become exciting and "forbidden fruit," you may want to train your kids in their *appropriate* use, by helping you to start a fire in the fireplace, light candles if the power goes out, etc. Sometimes competence can compensate for allure.
- Teach your kids that, in no uncertain terms, life is more important than any possession. Children (and adults alike) lose their lives by impulsively going back into the home for something that ultimately has little or no true value when compared to life itself.
- Do your own fire safety check. Pretend you're a fire inspector hired by your ex's lawyer to examine your premises for fire safety. That ought to inspire you.
- Have smoke detectors that actually work. Check the batteries and keep them fresh.
- Teach your kids "duck and cover" skills, and even have drills if you feel it necessary. They love it.
- Again, HAVE A PLAN. Teach your kids exactly how to exit the house in an emergency. Time and time again, experience has demonstrated that there is simply no substitute for training in these circumstances.

GENERAL MEDICAL CONCERNS

This is another one of these areas where we're going to make suggestions that you'd think any well-trained orangutan would take for granted. But, in point of fact, we're guilty of many of the same things that we're going to tell you are so stupid and ridiculous.

Before we confess, we have to explain a simple fact that has probably been hard-wired into the male genetic structure since time immemorial. We take no joy in this, but please pay attention.

Paleontologists, using the latest DNA techniques, have recently discovered that, as early as caveman days, males and females had glaringly different responses to medical events. The genetic female response to virtually any medical event was "Get on the mastodon, we're going to the doctor." However, it appears that the male's DNA programmed him to respond: "I don't know, let's sleep on it and see how he is in the morning. And by the way, pass me another rib, will ya?"

For example, Saffer was working with a man who by all accounts was a model noncustodial father. He was diligent, straightforward, invested in his kids, and an all-around great guy. He had his son and daughter for the weekend and took them on a long nature hike to enjoy the summer scenery in the nearby mountains. Coming down from a ridge they spotted a stream across a small plain, and raced across the plateau to reach it. When they reached the stream, the seven-year-old boy complained that he had hurt his ankle. Since he was not in obvious distress, dad thought that maybe he turned it a little or possibly got scratched by some briars while running across the field.

They made their way down the mountain to the car, and again, the boy complained that his ankle hurt, and in fact that it was swelling. Confident in his diagnosis of a slight sprain, "Dr. Dad" proceeded back to town and returned the kids to their mother. He dutifully told his ex of the child's complaints, and returned home. By the time he walked in the door of his apartment he already had a message from his ex on the answering machine. Hearing the boy's complaint she had immediately taken him to the doctor, where removal of his shoes and socks *revealed that in fact he had been bitten by a poisonous snake.* You can only imagine the rest of the story.

All of this is only to illustrate the critical importance of attending to issues such as these. Men as a rule don't take themselves to the doctor in the face of "minor" ailments or discomfort. And they impose this ethic on their children as well. *But you can't.* Even if you were still married to their mother, you would have to learn this lesson.

For example!—When McClure's kids were young, he had been working in the backyard garden, spraying flowers with some sort of insecticide. The telephone rang, he went in and answered it, one thing led to another (sandwich and a beer), and he ended up watching a baseball game while his kids played with a friend's kids out back.

Top of the third inning, tie game, the long-suffering Mrs. McClure runs into the den frantic because the youngest McClure was found entertaining the other children by spraying them with "some stuff" in a sprayer she found by the flower garden.

One call to the ER, one call to Poison Control, and several calls to the other children's parents rapidly ensued. The rest of the afternoon was spent disposing of clothes and bathing a group of children in various substances.

Stuff happens. Even to the, uh, best of us.

Take every medical event very seriously. Resist your natural, genetically predisposed inclination to "sleep on it" and see how it is in the morning. Use your judgment, to be sure, but when there is the tiniest shred of doubt, act as though your wife's attorney was in the next room. Get medical attention, even if in the end the pediatrician says all of the things you would have said. It's better coming from the doc than from you.

SAFETY FIRST—HERE IT IS AGAIN

- Keep a first-aid kit in the home and know how to use it.
- Talk to your child's pediatrician to get guidelines on when to take your kids in and when to handle it yourself.
- Take medical complaints seriously. Don't automatically doubt your kid's motivations. Even if it's a ploy for attention, it still means that your kid needs attention! Tend to the medical issue and then deal with how your kid may be seeking attention from you. But tend to the medical issue first.
- Don't take anything for granted. Just because you "toughed it out" when you were hurt, or just because you have a high pain tolerance or whatever, don't project this onto your kids.

- Above all, HAVE A PLAN FOR MEDICAL EVENTS.

OUTSIDE THE HOME

The way you prepare your child to deal with life outside the home is at least as important as the way you parent her inside your home.

First, the basics. The way you dress your child says volumes about your competence as a father. As we've mentioned once before, Mrs. McClure can drive by a bus stop in the fall and tell which kid is with his mother and which is with his father.

The kid who is with his mother will be dressed in clothes that *match*, for starters. Mothers have a fashion sense that often seems to escape fathers. They understand that stripes don't go with plaids. They understand that *plaids* don't go with plaids, for God's sake. And they know that when it's chilly outside you *make* your kid take a jacket with him. Even if he doesn't wear it, he's carrying it.

There seems to be a tendency for dads to overlook this kind of stuff. They tend to trust their kid's judgment (?!) about what "cool weather gear" actually means: a "cool" t-shirt and "cool" pants. No sweater. No jacket. Dads also seem to match clothes according to the "whatever rises to the top" system. It doesn't matter what goes together. It just matters that it's reasonably clean and it's there.

Well, this is OK under normal circumstances, but not when you're a single dad. You need to develop a better fashion sense for your kids. Watch other people's kids. Drive by bus stops and see what the kids look like. Look at catalogs of kid's clothing. Try to understand that this subject is much more important to

GUIDELINES FOR DEALING WITH
PEDIATRICIANS (PART 1)
BY MICHAEL DICKENS, M.D.

Do

- call the doctor's office early in the course of an illness for advice or for an appointment. You may not want to spend time during a weekend visitation at the doctor, but contacting the doctor early will save time and distress later.
- remember that the pediatrician is there to help your child, and will not consciously take sides in your marital situation. Let the doctor take care of your child; don't try to involve him or her in your situation.
- be honest with your child's pediatrician when you are confused or don't understand how to handle a problem. This is a sign of strength and concern on your part, not a sign of weakness that will be held against you in a future custody dispute.
- keep your feelings toward your ex under control when dealing with the pediatrician.
- always, *always*, treat the doctor's staff with respect and courtesy. It will get you far.

Don't

- assume any medical problem will simply "go away"— when in doubt, call the doctor.
- wait until the end of the day or Sunday night to call the pediatrician for something that has been ailing your child all day or all weekend. This may result in having to be seen by an on-call physician who is unfamiliar with your child's medical history.
- blame everything that's wrong with your kid on your ex.
- put the doctor in the middle of your problems with your ex
- use the doctor's bill as a means of retaliating against your ex. This doesn't help your child.
- forget that illnesses and medical treatments can be frustrating for everyone—don't take it out on the doctor.

your child (and likely to your ex) than it is to you.

Most importantly, dress your kids for safety. This is something you may really have to work at.

DRESS FOR SAFETY

- When your kids go outside, dress for the weather, and for the activity.
- Avoid drawstrings on clothing for the playground. These can catch on equipment or other things and harm your child.
- Make sure they wear helmets, knee pads, elbow pads, and any other safety equipment that is required for bicycle riding, skateboarding, hockey, soccer, etc. NEVER let them play organized sports without the proper safety gear.
- Never put their full names or address on "outside" articles, like bookbags, backpacks, lunch boxes, etc. Initials should do.
- Make sure that outerwear, like heavy coats, backpacks, etc., bears reflective strips so that they can be seen from a distance.

PRACTICE "NEIGHBORHOOD SKILLS"

- First, the basics. Make sure your kids know your full name, address, and telephone number. This is not their primary residence, you know. They don't see your full name and address very often. Your telephone number may be on "speed dial." Make sure they know all of it.

- Post emergency numbers and explicit directions to your house on a board right next to the telephone in case something should happen when you're out of the house.
- Talk to your neighbors. Find a neighbor willing to have their home be a "safe house" for your children in the event of an emergency. Make sure your kids know to go there *at the first sign* of something wrong.
- There are occasions when kids must be left at home on their own for a period of time. If you must be out while your kids are at home, even for just a few minutes, let someone know, and make sure you can be reached on a moment's notice in the event of an emergency.

PRACTICE "EMERGENCY SKILLS"

Make sure your child knows what to do should she become lost or separated from you:

- Teach your young child about "helping persons"—police, firefighters, store owners, anyone in a uniform.
- Teach them that if you're separated, they must (1) find a "helping person"; (2) have the helping person contact you, your ex, or a "safe neighbor"; and (3) stay with the helping person until someone you know arrives.

PRACTICE "STRANGER SKILLS"

Finally, make sure your children know full well who is a friend, neighbor, and "helping person" and who is not. Don't scare them, but assertively teach them the following:

- Make sure they know what a "stranger" is, as opposed to neighbors, friends, or "helping persons."
- Teach them the "No Secret" rule: No one who is truly a friend, neighbor, or helping person would ever ask a child to "keep a secret" from her parents. No one.
- Talk frankly about private parts, using the appropriate terminology (no slang and no cutesy-wutesy terms, please).
- Teach your child to be suspicious of adults who:
  - want to play a game with them;
  - want them to help "look for something";
  - want to "show them something";
  - offer candy, popular toys, etc., to them;
  - claim to be a friend of either Mom or Dad; or
  - get too close to them, invading their physical space.
- Above all, teach them to trust their instincts. Teach them that if they have an inner feeling, a gut sense, that something is wrong, dangerous, or somehow "fishy," they are to leave and find you, your ex, a neighbor, or the nearest "helping person."

The Mundane Is Important:
Homework, Chores, and Other Drudgery

It's unfortunate that we have to call this "visitation." It seems to suggest that you're going to your aunt's house or something. When you're at your aunt's house you have to behave yourself, but you don't have to do a lot of the things that you're expected to do at home. Unless your aunt is like Cruella DeVille from *101 Dalmations*, you don't ever have to vacuum her house, do her dishes, wash out her sink, or fold her laundry. And she is expected to wait on you, the burden for your comfort is all hers. Because you're a *guest*. You're just *visiting*.

But your kids aren't guests. They're not "just visiting." Your ex may view it that way. But they're not. And don't you ever fall into the trap of thinking that they are, either. They're in *their other home*, the one in which they are parented by their father. This means that they are not guests. They are children. They have responsibilities to the household. Just because they're not there all of the time doesn't mean that they don't have a crucial role in the operation of the household. Quite the contrary. Part of your job is to make them feel that they have a strong sense of ownership in your home. Because it's their home, too.

So don't be bashful. Punish them if they do wrong. Reward them if they do right. And give them responsibilities and ownership in the operation of your home. *Their* home. That means chores.

CHORES

Chores are very important. They teach responsibility, pride in a job well done, allegiance to you and to their own belongings, and a host of other good lessons. Kids will resist them. It's their nature. It's what they do. But chores are important in the long run, so you know what you have to do. Here are tips for winning the "Chore Wars."

- Select a reasonable number of chores. Don't overload the kids; they're not slaves. So give them a reasonable amount of responsibility.

- Select chores that your child is actually capable of doing. It's probably not reasonable to ask a six-year-old to make the bed on her own. Most six-year-olds can't even reach across the bed. They're just not equipped to do a good job of this. Make sure the chores are age-appropriate.
- Operate the chores on a schedule. Give your child a reasonable time frame in which to complete them. Don't interrupt a favorite TV program or any other activity to have the child do a routine chore. Expect it to be done by a certain time. Provide reminders if necessary, but don't nag.
- Inspect the child's work to make sure that the chore was done responsibly. Not perfectly, responsibly. Build in incentives for a job particularly well done to help them take pride in their work.
- *Model* the behavior you expect them to show by doing your own chores in a timely, responsible, and cheerful manner. It's the only way you'll have any credibility for reprimanding them when they don't.

HOMEWORK

This may well be one of your most daunting challenges. You wouldn't believe the number of parents we see whose entire households are disrupted because of homework. There seem to be several causes. First, it does seem that schools are giving kids more homework, and at earlier ages, than in days gone by. Second, many teachers don't adequately prepare youngsters for homework, and often use homework for new learning. Finally, many parents simply employ poor strategies to get homework accomplished.

Homework *is* unpleasant. And if you're anything like either of the authors, you hated it when you had to do it. One of the things we know for sure about children is that they tend to detest anything that's boring, repetitive, tedious, mundane, and detail-oriented. And we defy you to find anything about homework that's *not* any and/or all of the above. Homework is usually practice work, aimed at mastery. Hence the 30 sentences or 40 math problems, when we all know that just one or two might do.

But you still have to make sure the homework gets done, and that it gets done reasonably well. And you may not feel comfortable helping your child. It may well be that you were a lousy student, and you may have legitimate difficulties with the material that your child is studying. This we completely understand. English is like a second language to Saffer, and McClure, having taken geometry three times in high school, still couldn't pass it to this day. This is in large part why we're psychologists and not editors or mathematicians. So, if your kid needs help and you don't understand the subject matter, don't despair. Model good problem-solving skills by finding someone who does have familiarity with the subject matter and enlist their help.

"HOMEWORK WARS" – 10 WAYS TO WIN

1. Come to an understanding with your child that homework will be done every night. Model for your child that

this is important and that it takes precedence over other things.

2. Set aside a specific "Homework Time," and try very hard not to deviate from this. Kids need routine, especially for distasteful things like homework. Stick to it—even if it means that you have to tape one of your favorite shows and watch it later. Be consistent.

3. Provide your child with a quiet, non-distracting environment in which to do homework. No TV, radio, etc., until homework is done. Be around to supervise and be available to help.

4. Have all necessary supplies—pencils, paper, etc.—on hand and easily accessible. It's hard enough to have to do this stuff. Don't make it worse.

5. Have a good enough relationship with the teacher or with other parents so that you know who to call in the event that the assignment is lost or forgotten.

6. Try to get your hands on an extra set of books, so that homework never has to be left undone because the necessary book is at mom's house, at school, etc.

7. Be on hand to supervise, monitor, and help. Be patient, understanding, and remember what it was like when you were a kid. If the two of you together simply can't get something, defer until later. Write a note to his teacher to let her know that a sincere attempt was made. But make sure that the effort is there.

8. Check the work to make sure it's done reasonably well. Make sure it's *reasonably* neat. Don't expect perfection, and don't impose your standards on the teachers. She

knows what fourth-grade handwriting looks like. If it's acceptable to her, it should be acceptable to you.

9. Avoid the temptation to use homework time to impress your kid with how smart you are, or to prove to your ex what a hard case you can be. First, you'll probably just end up looking like a jerk. Second, it's not necessary. Just make sure it gets done, and make sure you're there to monitor and provide help if necessary. It *is* just homework, after all.

10. Make homework time compelling. Make it worth your kid's while to get it done, and to get it done reasonably well. Plan fun activities to be done after homework is completed. Have good snacks to celebrate the timely completion of homework. Anything you can do to help make it in your kid's interest to approach homework with a good attitude and work ethic will serve her well in the long run. It'll make your life a lot easier, too.

OTHER DRUDGERIES (THE MUNDANE IS IMPORTANT)

We all remember that as children we were forced to do things we disliked. We had to go to religious services regularly, even when we thought them "boring" at best. We had to go to our grandparents' house, where we had to be polite and endure listening to seemingly endless adult conversations that had no relevance to us at all. We had to go to family reunions, full of people we didn't know, or people we'd heard the worst sorts of gossip about all year. We'd watch our parents be nice to them, and wonder what was so great about being a grown-up if you had to do stuff like that. Or

GUIDELINES FOR DEALING WITH
YOUR CHILD'S SCHOOL
BY MACK TATE, ELEMENTARY SCHOOL PRINCIPAL

Make sure the school has the proper documentation to honor your rights with regard to your child. Schools may need copies of divorce decrees, custody papers, etc., in order to allow you on the premises, and to be able to provide you maximum access to your child.

Make arrangements to receive copies of all correspondence from the school regarding your child, including report cards, announcements, newsletters, etc. Provide self-addressed stamped envelopes to facilitate this, if necessary.

There is no substitute for communication. Communicate with the school and with your child. Don't hesitate to write notes to the teacher, and do anything else you can to stay informed.

Read the school handbook. This provides a better understanding of the school's philosophy, and also allows you to help your child with questions about rules, regulations, and so on.

Support your child's schooling and keep the school a neutral place. Avoid bringing your conflicts into the school.

Attend all parent conferences. Make a list of questions to ask the teacher about homework, curriculum, projects, etc. Ask for input from the teacher and be receptive and nondefensive. Some schools ask that both parents attend conferences. If so, do this with dignity.

Take some time to meet with other school personnel (guidance, physical education, art, etc.) who work with your child.

Volunteer. Chaperone a field trip, assist with Back to School Night, etc. Volunteer in the classroom or in the library. Become a presence in the school.

Join your child for lunch in the school cafeteria whenever possible. Cafeteria food really isn't bad.

we had to visit sick neighbors and take them food—even though it was boring, and maybe a little weird. Or we had to go to boring civic functions because one of our parents was involved. There were any number of things we had to endure.

But you know what? As miserable and boring as these things were, we tend to look back on them fondly as adults. Partly because they were the "right" things to do. And partly because there's something of value to be had in all of these experiences, whether you realize it as a kid or not. Even if it involves some small sacrifice. Or perhaps *because* they involve some sacrifice. It helps you to see over and above your own narrow self-interests. It helps you to be less self-centered, and it helps you to see the value in doing things for other people for a change. All important lessons for kids to learn.

So, if you are involved in things like this, things that appear to be mundane and "drudgery," don't hesitate to involve your kids. If they protest, involve them anyway, under protest. And if they complain to their mom and she tries to use it against you, simply explain it and press on. It's the right thing to do.

FRIENDS, SCHOOL, AND LIFE OUTSIDE THE HOME

As your children grow older, they will become more and more involved in activities outside of the home—not just your home, but your ex's home as well. This is natural, and should be encouraged, even though it lessens your time with them. Because it's not about how much time *you* get to spend with *them*—it's about having them enjoy a good, healthy, and above all, normal childhood.

174

A goal we've aimed for throughout this book, even though we haven't addressed it explicitly, is for your child's upbringing to be as similar as possible to the way it would be if you and their mother could have remained married.

In an intact marriage, when the child begins to develop friendships outside the home and immediate neighborhood and gets invited, for example, to a sleepover, the first question is not "Does this sleepover fall on *my* time?" Yet we'd bet money that this is the very first consideration in 95% of divorced households. When a child shows talent at the piano and wants to take lessons and perhaps play in an ensemble that meets twice a week for practice, it never dawns on *married* parents to figure out who gets "cheated" out of time with the kid as a result. Logistics may be addressed, of course, but not "whose time" gets cut.

In fact, in many intact family situations, by the time the child reaches mid-adolescence, his time with either parent is at a bare minimum. Between school, sports, after-school activities, homework, and part-time jobs, coupled with your own responsibilities and obligations, your child will actually not see all that much of you. And this is good. This is as it should be. So you make sure that, at this age, you "schedule in" time with your kids. And you make sure it's time well spent.

Do's and Don'ts of Managing Your Child's Life Outside the Home

DO

- Encourage and support your child's healthy activities. Provide financial support, emotional support, and moral support.

- Provide transportation and logistical help whenever possible, and help to defray expenses if at all possible, even if it's not the activity you would have chosen.
- Encourage your child to practice piano, baseball, tuba, ballet, or whatever activity it may be, even though the practice occurs on "your time." Even if your ex enrolled him in tuba lessons without your notification or consent.
- Allow your child to go to sleepovers, even if they're on "your time." To get some time with them you might have to do things like pick her up a little early the next morning before she goes back to her mom.
- Volunteer to be an assistant "den mother" for his Cub Scout pack—hey, whatever it takes. If it means having her invite her friends over to *your* house for sleepovers, all the better. You might even have some fun.

DON'T

- Deny your child opportunities for good, wholesome activities. Instead, encourage them at every turn.
- Resent the time these activities take away from you. Instead, involve yourself in the activity as much as possible to share in the experience (in a non-intrusive manner, of course).
- Make appeals to your ex, lawyer, child or anyone else for "make-up" time, for the time you may have missed because of these activities. Parenting is sometimes painful and it always involves sacrifice. It's part of growing up. For you as well as for them.

- Make your child feel guilty—*ever*—for the time these activities take away. Doing these activities is far healthier than staying home with a pitiful, morose soul who pouts, whines, and otherwise "guilt-trips" a child about "his" time.

Not having primary custody tends to make you very protective, even jealous, of your time with your kids. While this is a natural tendency, it also suggests that you may be looking through the wrong end of the telescope. What we're really interested in is not the time you have with your child. Rather, it's the time your child has with you. And when your child's normal, healthy activities begin to encroach on *your* time, what you're experiencing are the growing pains of normal development.

You do have an excuse, however, because you've been deprived of knowing exactly what *does* happen as a natural function of growth and development in an intact home. So talk with friends, family, and others who have raised children in an intact marriage. They'll help you get a more balanced, natural perspective on time with your kids. It's precious, to be sure. And limited. But it's really *their* time with *you*. It's their time. It has to be used to promote *their* growth and development. Not your need to be with them.

Trying to replicate a normal, intact household offers many advantages. In an intact home, when a father can get off early from work and the home team is in town, he calls his kid from the office and tells him to get his hat and glove and be ready to leave in 30 minutes. And the kid's ready in 15. In an intact marriage, when the business lunch is cancelled, at breakfast you tell your daughter you'll have lunch with her at school. And she finds herself beginning to look out the window by second period—just to see if you're there yet. If your sales seminar is over early, you slip by and pick the kids up from school.

There are thousands of other things that dads in intact marriages simply do and take for granted—without anybody ever telling them that they can't do it because it's not on "their time." But not you. You have to shed blood, sweat, and tears for these things—*if* you get to do them at all. We can't control your ex. If we could, we would let her know how important these things are. We can't intercede on your behalf and convince the Court, either, that these little things are the things parenthood is made of.

But we know one thing. If you are selfishly protective of *your* time with your kids—if you resent their outside activities that impinge on *your* time—if you cling to the belief that these things are part of a great conspiracy on the part of your ex to keep you away from *your* kids—and if you pout, whine, sulk, and otherwise carry on to make your kid feel guilty about outside activities and interests—if you do these things—it's a sure bet you will never be able to achieve "normalcy" in your relationship with your kids.

Your best shot at this goal is to handle these issues with dignity, maturity, and in a manner that clearly demonstrates to all that without question you have the best interests of your children at heart. You don't have any allies. Your ex isn't interested in this. Nor is her lawyer. The judge could not care less. Your only potential allies are your kids, and *only* if you handle it correctly.

If you handle your end of things right, *they* will be the ones requesting to have you pick them up whenever you can. And *they'll* be the ones demanding that they be allowed to have lunch with you at school whenever you have the free time. And *they'll* be the ones questioning why you can't pick them up when you're off early and the circus is in town, even if it's not "your day." But only if you do what you need to do, and do it right.

10
YOU AND YOUR EX
Becoming a Gentleman

Pound on an empty beer keg and you get a loud—but hollow—sound. Tap on a full keg and the sound isn't as loud. Which would you rather have at your picnic? You've been through an experience that has emptied you out. You might be an empty, hurt man bellowing your fury at the sense of frustration, betrayal, and isolation that now dominates your life. But like the keg, you are more valuable and welcome when you're full.

If something hurts, like your appendix or a painful cyst, a physician can cut it out. Feelings, on the other hand, can't be cut out in an instant. The negative ones go away when you fill yourself up with things that give you pride, fulfillment, and pleasure. You can then bring joy to your weekend guests. Your children can now see you as a source of fun, playfulness, and support.

Only a poor host would invite his guests to an empty keg party.

WE KNOW IT'S NOT A "RELATIONSHIP"... SO WHAT THE HECK IS IT?

Obviously, marriage is a very complex and challenging relationship. The divorce rate attests to this fact. And you have firsthand personal knowledge of what a difficult relationship marriage can be. Yours did not survive these challenges. However, when it comes to complexities, the marriage relationship can't hold a candle to the "divorce relationship."

This relationship is so difficult, in fact, that we can't even develop a word for it. We have terms for every other form of intimate relationship, from "housemates" to "lovers" to "commitment partners" and any number of other designations. But no word for your relationship to your ex. Your relationship to her is only defined by what it is *not*: "*former* spouse," "*ex*-husband," "*estranged* husband," etc.

Our job here is to help you define this new role in more positive ways, even if we can't come up with an appropriate term for it. As always, we want you to get active and take positive, affirmative steps toward managing this relationship. Your marriage to this woman, at least in the beginning, was a relationship based on love, trust, shared goals, and not a small measure of animal lust. The divorce relationship, by its very nature, cannot be based on these things. In the typical divorce, love has diminished (or even been eclipsed by hate), trust has been shattered, goals are divergent, and, even if lust remains, any expression of it would be disastrous.

We're not asking you to "work together," to "reconcile your differences," or to "mediate conflicts in your relationship." If the two of you could do this, odds are you'd still be married. We're not asking you to love her again, or even like her again. We're not asking you to renew your relationship with her or give in to her whims. What we're asking is that you construct your relationship with her in ways that enhance *your children's chances* of feeling safe, secure, and cared for.

We're not operating under any delusions here. We don't anticipate that this will be a cooperative endeavor by any stretch of the imagination. We have no confidence at all that she can set aside her own hurt, anger, and spite to truly work cooperatively with you.

And frankly, we're not too sure about you, either. That's why we stress again and again that your job is to control the things you can control and adjust to the things you can't. So, you can't put forth a half-hearted effort and then quit because "she didn't cooperate" (said with a distinctive whine). We can't expect her to cooperate. You can't hinge the future of your involvement with her and your children on whether or not she cooperates. You can only take responsibility for your own actions and your part of the relationship.

Remember, you're not doing this in isolation. You have quite an audience. It's not a particularly friendly audience at that. You have your ex. If she had confidence in your parenting ability and your competence as a husband and father . . . well, you know the routine. There's her lawyer, who may well be sending his kids to college on your divorce and custody issues. There's the judge, who's probably not too sure of you, either. There are the in-laws, and God only knows what they think of you. And then there's the most important audience of all, your children.

Obviously, it would be our hope that you conduct yourself in a dignified, mature manner simply because it's the right thing to do. Or because you understand that indeed "living well is the best revenge." But, if you can't conduct yourself responsibly for these noble motives, at least do it for your children. Because they're watching. And they see, hear, and understand a lot more than we give them credit for.

They're watching this drama unfold, and they have a big stake in the outcome. Their security and future development hinge on a positive outcome, even if the two players cannot live together and may not even like one another. And your child loves you, warts and all. She loves her mother, too.

SHE'S A SINGLE PARENT NOW, TOO, YOU KNOW

A brief word about your ex. She's a single parent, too. And she's probably never been a single parent before. Even if this is the way she wanted it, this is new to her, too. And it's hard.

She's dealing with a failed marriage. She has to face others, too. Friends, parents, other relatives, your friends. And it's uncomfortable for her as well. So, even if she was the motivating force behind the divorce, she's finding herself under a great deal of stress. And, even if you believe to the core of your being that it serves her right, feeling that way doesn't help your kid.

So, again, we're not asking for your sympathy. We just want you to be aware that this is not easy for her, either. No matter what she says. In any case, this is not about her. It's about your kid. And it is in your kid's interest for you to understand that his mother is in a tough situation. A new and stressful situation, with fears, anxieties, and uncertainty. And anything that increases her stress and discomfort will ultimately affect him.

This is a most important point—because we're going to be asking you to do things that are likely inconsistent with the way you feel about her. We live in a pretty coarse age, where sayings like "Nice guys finish last" and "Don't get mad, get even" too often form the basis of our approach to conflict resolution.

If she and you were the only two people involved, we suppose that you would be free to adopt this approach. But there are others involved—your kids. And for them, it's not about "finishing first" or "getting even." They're just trying the best they can to adjust to a difficult situation. Because of this, your job is to construct a relationship with your ex that helps *them*. Even if it means swallowing your pride at times, and even if it means behaving in ways that are contrary to the way you feel. And we understand that the ways you feel can be pretty intense.

THE POWER OF BETRAYAL

Your relationship to this woman, this woman who carried your children, is the most complex of all human relationships. More complex now even than the marital relationship. Because while she was once your wife, she is no more. She is no longer your confidante, but she once was. She was your "soulmate"; she understood you. Now she feels she hardly knows you.

She may well know more about you than anyone else on the planet. The bad along with the good. You placed your trust and faith in her. Trust that she would never hurt you. That she would never use your "secrets" against you. Faith that she would be there for you (in sickness and health and all that stuff, right?). She was your bed-mate in the most intimate of ways. But no more. She's really not your enemy, but she's certainly not your friend, either. You share a past together, but not a future. Except that you also share children, in whose future the two of you do have a common interest.

As human beings, we experience an extremely broad range of emotions. Take a few minutes and think of the sheer number of terms we have available to identify different emotional states. Frustration, irritation, anger, rage, fury, on the negative spectrum; contentment, pleasure, happiness, exuberance, joy, on the positive spectrum. Just to name a few.

As we develop, our experience introduces us to the emotions that correspond to all kinds of situations. As children, we learn about frustration and disappointment early, as we discover that our every need won't be met. Through academic and competitive experiences we learn about pride, dignity, aggression, diligence, and more. As teenagers we begin to learn about infatuation, "puppy love," the pain of separation and loss, and finally true love. Throughout our development we have "on-the-job training" to help us understand and manage a wide range of emotional states.

Except for one. There is one particular set of emotions that cannot be experienced as a child. It takes adult experience. Further, it takes *intimate* adult experience. This emotional experience is the experience of betrayal.

We tend to use the word "betrayal" in a variety of circumstances involving trust and loyalty. We say someone "betrayed our trust" or a friend "betrayed" us by forming different loyalties. But these forms of betrayal, while strong, do not come close to the power of the real thing.

True betrayal—deep betrayal—requires intimacy. Not just sexual intimacy, although this is a critical ingredient in any recipe for betrayal, but emotional intimacy, trust at the most fundamental level, where you actually give over part of yourself, entrusting it to another. As in marriage. No emotional experience comes anywhere near this level of betrayal in terms of its destructive impact.

Just think about it. Read your newspaper, watch the news, and see how many murders are committed by "an estranged husband." How many murder-suicides occur in the context of separation and divorce. How many spouses are killed or injured upon discovery of an illicit affair.

In all of our collective years of practice, we have seen nothing that even comes close to betrayal in driving sick behavior. Nothing can cause an otherwise rational and sane man to lose his dignity as suddenly or as dramatically. Nothing else can cause an otherwise calm and sensitive woman to become a fire-eating monster like betrayal. And unlike many emotional experiences, betrayal just doesn't go away. It doesn't diminish with time, like anger or disappointment. It lingers, and often seems to grow ever more pernicious and malignant. And it particularly lingers when the source of this betrayal continues to play a role in your life—in fact, not only to play a role, but to remain in your life in ways that are not under your control. This is tough stuff we're talking about.

So, if betrayal is active and alive in your relationship with your ex, as it is in most divorces, there are some things you need to do:

If You're the Betrayer

- Understand what you've done—don't get all defensive, just take an honest look at it and take responsibility for it. Don't blame *her* for what *you* have done.
- Have an appreciation of how much you've hurt her—she trusted you, she counted on you, and she had children with you. And you have damaged her.
- Accept the fact that you're going to have to deal with this with your kids. She can't keep her hurt from them, and she's not going to protect you by keeping them in the dark.
- Try to understand some of her actions in the light of your betrayal. It doesn't excuse them, but it helps to make sense out of them.
- Make things right—not by apologizing (although that wouldn't hurt), self-flagellation, or any other attempts at atonement. Make things right by being constantly vigilant and diligent about doing the right thing. At all times. Under all circumstances. If people are predisposed to see you in a certain light (and you have brought this about), you have to work all the harder to behave in ways that disprove their preconceptions.

If You're the Betrayed

- Remember that there was a time when she was the best thing that ever happened to you. She was warm, thoughtful, caring, sensitive, and exciting. That's why you married her. And that's why you decided she would be the mother of your children.

- Remember that she's the same person. Circumstances have changed, and she's done some rotten things, but she's still the same person.

- Begin to understand why the betrayal affected you so strongly. Was it an insult to your narcissism? To your manhood? To your pride? Try to understand the power of your reaction.

- Put your feelings in proper perspective and don't let them propel sick behavior on your part—it'll only hurt your kid.

- **Make things right—we know, we know, that's also what we said to do if you were the Betrayer. But we can't tell her to make things right. She's not reading this book, you are. You need to make things right by managing your emotions so that they don't interfere with your job of raising your kid . . . *with her.***

VISITATION AND YOUR EX

Visitation is tough. You have to go to your ex's home (maybe even your own house) to get your children. Children who, you are convinced, would be much better off with you, anyway. And you have them only for a specified period of time. And it's never enough. Then you have to take them back when you're told. Not when you're finished with your activities. Not when they're ready. And certainly not when *you're* ready. What's more, all of this has been dictated by someone who probably doesn't even know your kids.

However, by now you probably know what we're going to tell you. As always: Be honest, be straightforward, and do what you say you're going to do, *when* you say you're going to do it.

There's a tremendous temptation to play around with visitation pick-up and drop-off times. Transition times tend to be anxious times, anyway. You can *really* irritate your ex by showing up an hour early to pick up your kids. You know, hang around, try to weasel your way into the house, see what's going on in there, see if there's anything incriminating you can pick up on. Especially if you know it makes her nuts to have you in the house. Yeah, yeah, even if it's *your* house.

You can also make your ex crazy by bringing the kids home late. You have to time it right, though. If you're too late, she might just get a Show Cause order against you. If you're not late enough, it's just rudeness. But if you can time it somewhere in between, you can really make her looney tunes. Especially if she has somewhere to go . . . say, to work, her mother's, or, dare we say it, on a date.

Yep, you can ruin her entire weekend with these kinds of stunts. You can make her as angry as she has made you. And make her feel as helpless as you feel. You don't even really have to put much effort into it. Just be late. And don't call.

But of course, you *do* have an audience for all of this. Your child knows what time it is. She knows what time she was supposed to be home. She may even have had plans or obligations of her own this evening. She knows her mom will be in a rotten mood when they get home. Because you were late. And she knows that her evening may also be ruined. Because you were late.

Then there's clothes, toys, and other stuff. You wouldn't

believe (at least we *hope* you wouldn't believe) the conflicts we have seen over issues related to clothes, toys, and other belongings. Returning your child home in dirty or soiled clothes will cause a firestorm. Keeping some of the clothes that your ex sent with your kids will get even more of a reaction.

Of course, clothes, toys and stuff actually belong to your child, and not to you *or* your ex. You show respect for your child by respecting his belongings. By keeping his clothes clean and available to him. By taking care of his toys and making sure that he has his toys available to him no matter what house he's in at any given time. By showing respect to his belongings, you show him respect. If you use his things as weapons against his mom, you teach him very different lessons indeed.

We could go on and on, but you get the picture. If you don't think you have enough time with your kids, there are ways to address this issue. Abusing the time that you do have with them is a lousy strategy. *What* you do during your time with your kids has been covered elsewhere. *How* to manage it vis-a-vis your ex will best serve the interests of your kids if you follow these simple guidelines:

VISITATION AND YOUR EX: 10 KEYS

1. Pick your kids up on time and in good humor.
2. Don't use transition times as an opportunity to irritate their mom.
3. Work on having a joyful time and return them to their mom in good spirits.
4. Respect their belongings and show them proper care.
5. Make scheduling changes way in advance.
6. Accept NO for an answer when your request for something special is denied. You don't call all the shots.
7. Keep appropriate boundaries between you and your ex.
8. Don't let your feelings toward their mom intrude on your time with them.
9. Be mindful of the clock and of your children's other commitments.
10. Above all, have fun and make the most of the time you have with them.

OR, BETTER YET:

THE TEN COMMANDMENTS OF VISITATION

Thou shalt have the interests of your children at heart at all times, and no other interests before them.

Thou shalt not have any images (work, personal problems, etc.) interfere with your children's time with you.

Thou shalt not take their mom's name in vain.

Thou shalt remember visitation and keep it sacred— free from interference by things unrelated to your relationship with your children.

Thou shalt honor the children's father *and* mother.

Thou shalt not kill their images of their parents as good, honest, and caring people.

Thou shalt not commit "girlfriend" in their presence, unless she's going to be their stepmom.

Thou shalt not steal their stuff to irritate their mom.

Thou shalt not bear false witness against their mom, or anybody else, for that matter.

Thou shalt not covet their relationship to your ex and her family.

CHILD SUPPORT

Now you *know* what we're going to say about child support. Like a lot of people, we have mixed feelings about this subject. But it is a man's sacred duty to provide for his children. It's just that the *mechanism* for providing for your children under these circumstances can be kind of screwy.

It's an awful lot to ask of a man. You award primary custody of his children to his ex. The one person on earth about whom he has raw and powerful negative feelings. And, in doing so, you take away a significant amount of his access to his own children. His freedom to exercise his parental role. You give over control of this part of his life to a woman who, at best, has little use for him, and, at worst, despises him. And then, *and then* . . . you tell him that he has to send her money every month! He has to write her a check and give over significant portions of his own hard-earned money to her. It's no wonder so many men use child support payments as a weapon against their ex-wives.

But this is the absolute wrong way to look at this issue. Your child support payments must be seen as separate from the divorce, custody, and all of those other issues. Child support is exactly what it says it is. It is your method of honoring your sacred commitment to provide for your children.

The last thing on earth you should do is to monkey around with child support payments. For a moment, just put yourself in your ex-wife's position. You have the children for the majority of the time. Whether you will admit it or not, you are engaged in a constant "competition" with your ex-husband to prove to your kids that you're the better parent. Your ex-husband has to make child support payments. This is money to support his children—it's *their* money (at least in theory). And then he doesn't make these payments. Or he makes them three weeks late. Or in installments of his own making. What a gift! What a great weapon in the "Who's the Best Parent" wars. And not only that, but the law, the police, and the sentiments of an entire nation are on her side. You're a DEADBEAT DAD! Great, huh?

So, if you just can't bring yourself to be responsible with the child support payments because it's your sacred duty, at least do it because you will simply look terrible if you don't. Besides, it's the right thing to do. If you have legitimate concerns that the money you're sending to your ex is not contributing to the well-being of your children, then you have an *obligation* to seek a remedy to this situation. Through appropriate channels.

But, we have to tell you, we've known our share of single mothers in our time, too. And it is exceedingly rare to see a woman who fritters away her child's support payments. Even though the amount may seem extreme and even punitive to you, typically these payments don't even come close to what it *really* takes to support a kid these days (unless you're Donald Trump, and in that case you'd never miss the money, anyway).

So, be a man. Separate the child support from the other issues in your relationship with your ex. See it as a sacred trust between you and your children. As an acceptance of your responsibility as a father to provide for them. In the long run, it's actually an honor, you know. And one that your kids will come to appreciate, in due time.

VACATIONS, SPECIAL OCCASIONS, AND OTHER HEADACHES

For some reason, vacations, special events, and other unusual circumstances tend to cause problems in the visitation. This is because they typically fall outside the "letter of the law" in terms of the Visitation Order. And, as such, they tend to be fair game for mischief, passive-aggressive behavior, and general irritation.

If you don't have primary custody and she does, then you have to understand that, as a general rule, you're at her mercy. We don't like it, you don't like it, and virtually nobody likes it . . . except her, perhaps. But that's the way it is.

Our general advice is to try to avoid special circumstances as much as possible. But sometimes you can't. If your company only gives you vacation time during a certain time frame, that's when you have to take it. And your ex should be expected to make every effort to accommodate this, as this is truly a special circumstance. If you have a rotating work schedule and variable free time, your ex is expected to make the appropriate accommodations.

But there is special and then there is special. And you have to be careful about what you term as "special." Going to your girlfriend's son's football playoff game may be special to you or to your girlfriend, but it really doesn't meet our criteria. Watching you play in a softball tournament doesn't really qualify. Now, going with you to a class reunion or other function where you can show them off to friends and family is much closer to our criteria. And your ex should be expected to make the necessary accommodations in these instances.

In our minds, however, there *are* some absolutes. Funerals, for example, absolutely meet our criteria. There is no good reason to prevent children from spending extra time with you to attend a funeral of a close loved one. Even if your children are too young to go to the actual service, they should accompany you in order to be with their extended family during such an important family time. Weddings, family reunions, and other significant family functions also absolutely meet our criteria. However, usually there is sufficient lead time to plan for these events and make the necessary compromises. Emergencies, such as serious accident or significant illness in the family, certainly qualify. You know how we feel about settling your differences in Court. But these circumstances would be exceptions. These are the few instances where we would support a trip back before the judge to settle the issue.

GRANDPARENTS, IN-LAWS, AND OTHER INTERESTED PARTIES

Grandparents should be a source of pleasure and comfort to children. We hope you have fond memories of your grandparents, for they are truly wonderful for a kid to have. They can love absolutely unconditionally, for they're not responsible for how the kid behaves. They can spoil a kid rotten, because they don't have to take him home. And they're just cool, like visitors from a completely different time and place. They have much to offer.

From a kid's perspective, they have cool stuff, and lots of times they're trying to get rid of their junk, so you get it. Only you don't think it's junk—to you it's a treasure. Their house smells different; not bad, just different. And they usually have treats there. Just for you. Stuff no mom in her right mind would let a kid get near, much less eat. And best of all, they think you're just as cute as you can be. Almost no matter what you do. They like you, and things that would drive your parents nuts they think are cute. Who could want more?

So keep this in mind when dealing with your former in-laws. Because while they may be your in-laws, they're your kid's grandparents. You're not related to these people, but they share the same blood as your children. All you shared with them was their daughter. Your children are part of them, just as surely as they're part of you and part of your parents.

These people may have sided with your ex during the separation and divorce. She may have sought solace in their home, and she may well have vilified you in their eyes. Remember, they had an obligation to be loyal to their daughter. Thus, they may have lots of negative feelings toward you by this time. They may not have even thought that you were the right man for their "little girl" in the first place, and may have been against you from the start. When you look at them, you may see evil incarnate. But your daughter sees her grandmother. And when they look at you, they may very well see a jerk. But when they look at your kids they see extensions of their very own lives into the future. No matter how you feel about them, you need to appreciate and respect how your kids feel about them. And how they feel about your kids.

If your kids are lucky, they'll have grandparents around for a long time to come. Which means that you still have to deal with them. With any luck, they'll attend most or all of your child's significant events. And you'll see them there. And you will have to interact with them for your kid's sake.

You will do your kids a great service by promoting their relationships with grandparents. Even if the ex in-laws don't reciprocate, you will help your children by modeling respect and a civil attitude toward their loved ones. Put yourself in your kid's shoes. If your son adores his grandfather, what must it do to him to hear you devalue this man? If your daughter reveres her grandmother, what must she think when you make ugly remarks about her? What kinds of loyalty conflicts will they experience if they are placed between you and their grandparents? The same respect is due here as to your ex, their mom. These days kids need all the adult support, attachments, and love they can get.

The golden rule for relating to your ex: never deprive your children of what they need just because of bad blood between the people they love.

11

SPECIAL CASES
Becoming Prepared

Pipes burst, roofs develop leaks, and potholes are seen on even the finest streets. No one can fault the homeowner or the highway department—until it becomes apparent that nothing is being done to alleviate the problems. It's the same within the family. Children develop problems. No one can blame you for that, but you must do something. You need to take care of business.

This chapter deals with the signs and behaviors that might call for help. It's important to know that you should gauge your success as a father not by whether or not your children develop problems, but by what you do to help when they occur.

Being a parent, especially a noncustodial parent, is tough enough under the best of circumstances. You get plenty of interference from those around you: courts, your ex, her attorney, perhaps even ex-in-laws and former friends. Often your hands are tied when you try to do even the most basic things. You certainly don't have the flexibility in parenting that custodial parents enjoy. You don't have the same latitude in making mistakes. Every mistake you make is apt to be amplified and perhaps distorted by an unforgiving audience. You have a great deal to manage, over and above the nuts and bolts of trying to parent your child.

Your task is difficult even when your situation is stable. When your kids are healthy and happy, when your family life is good, and even when your ex is being cooperative and understanding, parenting is still hard work. Noncustodial parenting is an especially fragile enterprise, fraught with uncertainty. In this chapter we prepare you for some of the more serious problems you might face.

PARENTING THE SPECIAL NEEDS CHILD

Physical handicaps are usually readily apparent, even to the casual observer. Treatments are fairly standard and support networks available. Developmental problems, however, tend to be more controversial and less universally accepted. They are often "invisible" disabilities. Their presence is not readily apparent, and the impact on the child can be serious, but subtle. Because they are often "invisible," they are more prone to be dismissed or explained away as moral shortcomings or character flaws. Children of divorce are often at risk for the development of certain of these difficulties. For these reasons, we will focus primarily on the developmental disorders in this section. Our advice for fathers of special needs youngsters, however, applies to fathers of *any* child with *any* type of disability.

These days physicians, psychologists, and child health professionals have become more sophisticated than ever in their ability to identify and treat conditions that may compromise a child's development. This is good. The better able we are to identify developmental problems, the better able we are to protect the child from their impact.

Of course, the other side of this coin is that more and more children are being diagnosed with "childhood disorders," and are then enrolled in "programs," receiving "services," or being treated with medication. For many reasons, some valid and some not, people have criticized this trend. But we have to err on the side of the trend this time. We've seen too many youngsters who have actually been helped a great deal by the identification and treatment of problems that, if left unidentified, would have harmed them in the long run. But, as always, we also advise caution, reason, and good old common sense when approaching this area.

ALPHABET SOUP

For some reason, the people who talk about these disorders can't stand to call them by their proper names, and instead opt for alphabetical shorthand. Usually when these disorders are referred to by "alphabet names," it shows they're being absorbed by the popular culture. This can be a danger sign, because it can also mean that the disorder is on the verge of becoming a fad. However, most childhood disorders in this alphabet soup actually do exist. While they may become faddish or get overdiagnosed from time to time, they really do tend to be legitimate problems, and are worthy of serious involvement on our part. Below is a listing of the most prevalent of these disorders.

EDUCATIONAL PROBLEMS

ALPHABET NAME (REAL NAME) AND WHAT YOU NEED TO KNOW

LD   (*LEARNING DISABILITIES*)   Learning disabilities are developmental problems involving deficits in the ability to acquire certain academic skills—reading, written language, math, and so on. They may be highly specific or very diffuse. They're typically diagnosed by school personnel with standard testing and involve no real "treatment," as such, but specialized educational strategies and accommodations have proven helpful.

ED   (*EMOTIONALLY DISTURBED*)   This term refers to a whole class of disorders. It's used primarily by schools, which provide special education services to children whose academic performance suffers from emotional difficulties. While schools can assign students to this category in order to receive Special Education services, they do not assign specific diagnoses of emotional disturbance.

MR   (*MENTAL RETARDATION*)   This is a third category of disorders that qualify for Special Education services through the schools. To warrant this designation, the child must obtain a score below a particular cutoff point on an individual IQ test *and* show significant problems with "adaptive behaviors"—self-care, hygiene, peer relationships, and so on.

A variety of disorders identified as impediments to academic learning have highly sophisticated names, which sometimes serve primarily to make the speaker of such names feel either important or highly educated. These are as follows:

HIGHLY SOPHISTICATED NAME:	WHICH MEANS:
Dyslexia	Can't read too well
Developmental Reading Disorder	See above
Dysgraphia	Can't write too well
Developmental Expressive Writing Disorder	See above
Dyscalculia	Can't do math too well
Developmental Math Disorder	See above
Developmental Articulation Disorder	Doesn't talk too well
Developmental Receptive Language Disorder	Doesn't hear too well

BEHAVIORAL DISORDERS

ADD /

ADHD (ATTENTION DEFICIT DISORDER)   Variously called "Hyperactivity," "Hyperkinetic Impulse Disorder," "Minimal Brain Dysfunction," "Attention Deficit Disorder," and "Attention Deficit/Hyperactivity Disorder." A pretty severe disability characterized by inattention, distractibility, and impulsivity significantly beyond the norm for a given age or stage of development. Perhaps the most overdiagnosed childhood disorder of all time. *But it does exist,* and can be highly debilitating if your child actually has it. Should be diagnosed only by a clinical psychologist, pediatrician, or child psychiatrist. Highly treatable, but treated with Schedule II medication. So, be careful and use common sense. If your kid really has it, cooperate with the treatment and do everything you can to help. If you have doubts, get a second opinion.

CD (CONDUCT DISORDER) Very serious childhood disorder diagnosed in children who show a number of alarming behaviors, which may include: cruelty to animals, setting fires, disregarding the physical safety of others, stealing, lying, and cheating, among other behaviors. They need immediate gratification, and engage in some or all of the above behaviors without the experience of guilt. Diagnosed primarily by psychiatrists and clinical psychologists. This is a serious diagnosis, and, if your child is assigned this particular diagnosis, you should certainly get a second opinion. These children tend to be dangerous, and tend to grow up to be individuals with sociopathic personality disorders.

ODD (OPPOSITIONAL DEFIANT DISORDER) Just what it sounds like. These kids are massive pains in the butt. Not just your run-of-the-mill pain-in-the-butt kid, but an *extraordinary* pain in the butt—to an extreme degree—all the time—regardless of who they're dealing with. To be diagnosed only by child psychologist or physician. Not to be confused with CD; ODD is much milder and far more amenable to treatments, usually behavioral in nature. Sometimes kids who experience traumatic events that are not under their control (like divorce) try to restore their sense of power and control inappropriately through this set of symptoms.

PDD (*PERVASIVE DEVELOPMENTAL DISORDER*) PDD encompasses the spectrum of autistic or autistic-like disorders. Pretty serious stuff, to be diagnosed only by a specialist (child psychiatrist, clinical psychologist, developmental pediatrician, child neurologist). Probably neurological in origin. Not to be assigned lightly. Indicates significant delays in many areas of development, but most particularly in the ability to establish and maintain appropriate communication and reciprocal relationships. Second opinions are highly encouraged.

MEETING THE CHALLENGE

Your role changes dramatically if your child has special needs over and above other youngsters of the same age. In addition to being the best parent you can possibly be, you now have a new duty to add to your job description. You now need to become the best *advocate* for your child that you can possibly be. This change brings significant challenges that you will have to deal with in order to truly help your child. There are basically three fundamental steps to becoming an advocate for your child:

STEP 1: DEAL WITH YOUR EMOTIONAL RESPONSE

There are few things more disturbing than finding that there's something wrong with your child. Something that sets her apart from the other children her age. Something that places her at a disadvantage. Something that's imperfect or deficient. Something that's wrong in a child whom you have held in your private fantasies to be perfection. Just as you did with the divorce, you need to mourn the loss of this image of perfection. You have to grieve and ultimately accept the reality. Denial may help you, but it doesn't help your child. If you're skeptical, don't hesitate to get a second opinion. But you must also be prepared to accept the second opinion, even if you don't like it.

You also must resist the temptation to assign blame. Parents often have a very strong need to make sure others know that *they* are not responsible for the difficulty in their child. This tendency is only heightened if you are in a contentious relationship with her mother—because then you have a vested interest in having it come from *her.* Again, though, while this may lessen your guilt or provide fodder in your "war" with your ex, it doesn't help your kid one bit. It will also only deepen the animosity between you and your ex. You're going to need her if you want to be in a position to really help your child.

STEP 2: BECOME AN EXPERT

Learn as much as you can about your child's difficulty. Particularly with the advent of the Internet, all the information you will ever need is right at your fingertips. Read everything you can find. Study the problem until you fully understand it. Understand how it may have come to pass. Understand its impact on your child's development. Understand how its impact may radiate out into other areas of your child's life (and yours as well). Learn about accepted treatments, their success rates, how they work, and why. And don't be afraid to look at alternative or unorthodox treatments. Don't rush out and embrace them, because most of them are bogus. But don't be afraid to look into them, either. Learn about the law and how the law applies to your child's particular difficulty. Learn about the Americans with Disabilities Act. Learn about Public Law 94-142, the special education law. Learn when and if your child may be entitled to certain benefits. Learn as much as you can about any laws that might affect your child's well-being.

Step 3: Advocate, Advocate, Advocate

Get out there and get to work. Make sure that everyone connected with your child is doing the absolute best they can. Make sure they're doing everything they're required to do.

Advocate for your child in the professional arena. Become a part of the treatment team. Stay in contact with the professionals. Educate them. You may well become better informed than they are in certain areas. Share new material with them. Ask them for material that they may have. But be tactful. Don't be a pain in the rear end, or it will screw things up.

Advocate in the community. Go to support group meetings. Talk with other parents in the same boat and enlist their help. Provide support to them, and allow them to provide the same support to you. See what's available in the community for your child. Wherever you can, fill in the gaps in what's available by advocating within the larger community.

Advocate in the school. Go to the school. Early and often. Talk with the special educators. Learn about their curriculum and methods. Sit in on classes where appropriate. Talk to people at the state level to make sure your particular school district is in compliance with state mandates and regulations. Don't play "gotcha," but do insist that the school be accountable for your child's education.

Advocate at home. Yes, and even work with your ex—two really *are* better than one, especially where your child is concerned. Work with your ex to provide the best possible environment for your child—to make transitions between the two homes less disruptive, to have consistent rule structures between the two homes, and to share the burden of parenting a challenging child.

Finally, learn to be *assertive* without being *aggressive*. Learn to be *persistent* without being *unreasonable*. Learn to be *knowledgeable* without being *arrogant*. Above all, learn to be *righteous* without being *self-righteous*.

PARENTING THE RESISTANT CHILD

SCENARIO #1

The telephone rings just as you're about to leave to pick up your son. It's his mom, and she says he's not feeling well. He's not feeling up to going with you today. This is the third time in a row he's been "sick," and you're beginning to get suspicious.

SCENARIO #2

You arrive at the house to pick up your daughter. As you round the corner you see your ex standing on the front porch, arms folded across her chest, and you know there's trouble afoot. She says your daughter is scared, crying, and refusing to go with you. And she's not about to *make* her go with you, either.

208

Scenario #3

Your kids spend the entire weekend complaining that they're "bored." There's nothing fun to do at your house. You don't do anything right, and even if you do, their mom does it better. And all their friends are in Mom's neighborhood. They hate "visitation." They want to stay at their mom's house, where things are the way they're *supposed* to be. So the next time you call, they're not at home and she says they don't want to come with you.

These moments cause unbridled anguish. And the pain that they cause is way out of proportion to what the particular situation would seem to warrant, because:

It serves as confirmation of your worst fears about your ex.
- She's causing the children to have the same feelings about you as she does.
- She really *is* spending all of her time brainwashing your children.
- She really *is* programming them to hate you.
- She really *is* highlighting all of your inadequacies to make you look bad.

It highlights you own insecurities.
- Maybe you really *are* a joke.
- Maybe you really don't have what it takes to be an effective dad.

- Maybe your ex was right all along.
- Maybe she really *is* a better parent than you, after all.

Perhaps worst of all, these events seem to place your ex in the dreaded "one-up" position.

Some of the most difficult times we've had in working with divorced families arise out of the types of scenarios described above. These situations stir powerful emotions on both sides. Obviously your ex has a vested interest in your child's resistance. Even though she may want the "night off" or have weekend plans, or truly desire for the kids to have a solid relationship with you, there is still some benefit to her when the kids have a problem with you. Because she's had problems with you, too. For your part, you've already been sensitized to rejection and criticism. You're already likely to be in a defensive posture.

The emotions stirred up by your child's resistance to being with you seem to call for instant action, a definitive statement from you. You're hurt, angry, and maybe just a little bit scared. When emotions of this intensity are stimulated, every pore in your body tells you you need to *do* something. You need to do something decisive, and you need to do it *now*.

We have the answer.

Through years of clinical training and experience, exhaustive reviews of scientific research, and extensive consultations with our colleagues, Saffer and McClure have developed a response strategy so dynamic, so creative, and so utterly ingenious that we should probably design our own website and market it. But, since we have no computer skills, and, since presumably

you paid good money for this book, we'll divulge the secret to
you here.

- **Do Nothing.**

- **Nothing.**

- **(Nothing.)**

Now, at first blush the simple elegance of this strategy may
escape you. It may seem like a copout or, worse, a surrender.
Here you are, poised for decisive action, and the best we can
do is tell you to do nothing? Okay, then, before we outline
this strategy in more depth, let's take a look at the possible
actions you could take in this situation, and list the possible
advantages of each.

STRATEGY	ADVANTAGES
Turn the situation into a confrontation. Don't budge. Do not accept what your ex is saying as fact. Assume she's lying. Make her "prove" that they really don't want to be with you. Place them squarely in the middle of the conflict if you have to.	—
Refuse to be denied. Bully your way into seeing or talking to your kids. Demand	—

that they talk to you or spend time with you, no matter what. After all, this is "your time," right?

Throw a tantrum. Rant and rave. Curse, spit, turn red. Tell her you don't believe her. In front of God and everybody. Even if she has to get her husband or call the police. Demand justice!

—

Retreat in anger. Relent and "give in," but make her pay. Make idle threats. Threaten her with court action, Show Cause orders, etc.

—

There you have it. If you think we've left out any advantages that we should add to our list, please let us know.

Clearly, if you explode you don't solve the problem. In fact, you become part of it—so much a part that you may end up obscuring the real problem. If you give in to your emotions—"follow your instincts"—you'll certainly do more harm than good. You'll also be setting a very bad example for your children. When your child refuses to talk to you or go with you, it's a difficult moment, to be sure. It's even more difficult when the messenger is your ex. But, difficult as it may be, it's not a crisis. It's not an emergency. It's a bump in the road—a long, long road.

Just like many of the other issues we have discussed, this is a challenge to you to take a lemon and try to make some lemonade. If you view this as a crisis, you will respond in "crisis mode."

If you view it as an insult to your manhood or fatherhood, you will respond in "macho mode." On the other hand, it you view this as an *opportunity*, as a chance to demonstrate your maturity, your parenting skills, and your competence, you will approach the situation quite differently. We would like for you to try and view this as an opportunity to model an appropriate response to stress for your children. An opportunity to give your ex confidence in your ability to work through difficult situations. And perhaps an opportunity to iron out some real difficulties in your relationship with your children.

So, train yourself to have an immediate response of "no response." Do nothing. Count to 10—or 50—or 100—whatever it takes. Collect yourself. Get a little distance from your emotional response. Get some perspective. Look at the big picture, "keep your eyes on the prize," and begin to develop a plan.

MAKING A PLAN

1. DEFINE THE PROBLEM

This is the first and most important step in attempting to solve any problem. If you turn the key to your car and nothing happens, you don't rush out and buy a new starter. You go through a series of steps to diagnose the problem. You check the battery, the cables, the solenoid switch, etc., and you find the source of the difficulty.

The same logic applies here. If you automatically define the problem as your ex, your goal then becomes to *win*. To defeat her. Your solutions will most likely be geared toward retaliating against her. Just for the sake of argument, consider that there really may be a problem somewhere not of your ex's making. Maybe your place *is* kind of boring. Maybe you *haven't* provided a "kid-friendly" place for your child. Maybe there's a genuine conflict in the relationship that you are not aware of. In order to do your child justice, you have to be willing to entertain the notion that there might actually be a legitimate reason for the resistance.

Maybe:

- Your child is legitimately sick when visitation time comes around—last time, too.
- Events with friends do conflict with the visitation.
- Something's happened at your home that was a legitimate source of discomfort.
- It's something about you.

Or perhaps there are other reasons that may seem less "legitimate," but which nevertheless require gentle, considerate handling rather than confrontation. For example:

- Your child is fearful of you or something in your environs.
- You really aren't any fun.
- He simply doesn't "feel like it" or it's too disruptive to him.
- She misses her mother too much to spend time with you.

2. Examine the Nature of the Problem

Try to understand the nature of the difficulty. Set your own hurt feelings aside and try to view the situation from your child's perspective. Try to understand, even if it only makes sense in "kid logic." Sometimes even the most bizarre things begin to make sense when you come to understand the context. Don't force the issue. Make an opportunity to talk to your child. Give your ex the benefit of the doubt and talk seriously with her, too. Because there are some difficulties that will require you to simply put your foot down and force your child to do certain things. You will need her help; she will have to support you when you put your foot down or you'll simply be putting your foot in your mouth.

Resist the temptation to jump to conclusions or to solve the problem immediately. Remember what things were like when you were a kid and how you might have felt in a similar situation. Keep an open mind and try to understand.

3. EXPLORE A RANGE OF OPTIONS

These are typically not "either/or" situations, where there is one and only one "right" answer. Usually there are a number of ways to come at a problem. At this point it may be helpful to discuss some possible options with your child and make her feel like she's part of the process. Be flexible. Be open to suggestions. Keep in mind that, in the long run, it's the *relationship* that's meaningful, not the setting, not the trappings. Your job is to do whatever you can reasonably do to ensure that the relationship develops in a healthy fashion. Even if it means that you need to make some changes. Even if it means that you spend your time in ways that you would not ordinarily choose. Even if it means that your ex may have been right about some things.

4. Set a Course of Action

Decide what you're going to do and how you're going to do it.
Set about doing it. If at all possible, include your ex in the plan.
But don't be impatient. Don't rush it. Allow things to unfold at
a natural pace, and usually they will fall into place.

5. Pat Yourself on the Back

Take pleasure in what you've done. You've taken what could
have been a catastrophe and turned it around. Even if the
situation doesn't end up exactly the way you would have preferred, you have averted a crisis. You have taught your kids
(and perhaps your ex) some important things, and you have
modeled appropriate behaviors. You have modeled impulse
control and restraint. You have provided a model for conflict
resolution. You have behaved in a mature, dignified fashion.
And you have kept your eyes on the prize. What more could
a kid want in a dad?

How to Know When Your Child's in Trouble

It's easy to tell if your car's in trouble. It makes noise, smokes,
shimmies and rattles, or it simply quits on you altogether. Or
your pet. When animals are in trouble they show real signs of
distress. They become sluggish and nonresponsive. In fact, *most*
things give pretty clear signals that trouble is afoot. Children do,
too, but sometimes you have to know what to look for.

If you've been paying attention at all, you've noticed that
children don't communicate the same way as adults. As any

parent of a teenager can attest, a smirk, a shrug, or a simple roll of the eyes can speak volumes. The simple word "whatever" can, by virtue of which syllable happens to be accentuated, mean variously "No way," "Yeah, sure, *right*," "So what," or "This conversation is over, you idiot." Even when they speak real English, we're still not always sure we "get it" half the time.

Kids often do have a wide range of communication tools at their disposal, but these all fail them when there's trouble. Part of the problem is simply developmental. These people aren't nearly as articulate as they would have us think. All of a sudden, even the most talkative and articulate youngster struggles when matters of the heart are involved.

If you don't believe us, the next time your kid looks down, just ask him to tell you what's wrong. You know the routine. If we were betting men (which we are), we would bet the ranch that you get:

a) "Nothing."

b) "I dunno." or

c) [shrug]

It's even worse when there's real trouble—when trauma has occurred, or when something bad is happening that they themselves don't even understand. In earlier chapters we talked about the importance of *being* with your child, of being attentive and sensitive, even when you're not directly engaged in conversation. And nowhere is this more important than in the context of being aware that something is wrong. Because your child is not going to sit you down and say:

Look here, Dad, I'm feeling kind of down because I just don't feel like a good person; I stay confused, I can't control my emotions half the time, and I feel hopeless and worthless. My friends don't seem to like me any more and I'm afraid that there's something so dreadfully wrong with me that I just can't bear to go on.

Nope. Even the most articulate child is not going to do this. The primary ways youngsters communicate that there's a problem are through *changes* in the way they do things. If you're not sensitized to the normal ebb and flow of your youngster, you'll miss the boat when something's not right. These changes can occur in several areas.

PHYSIOLOGICAL DISRUPTIONS

When bad things are happening, kids will often respond through their physical systems, showing a disruption in their normal biological functioning. While you shouldn't jump the gun at the first sight of any of these symptoms, be alert for a *pattern* of these behaviors. For example:

THE CHILD YOU KNOW:
shows a relatively normal sleep pattern—
- goes to sleep at a consistent time;
- gets to sleep relatively easily;
- sleeps throughout the night;
- generally wakes up rested and *looks* rested in the morning.

shows a solid, pretty consistent appetite—

- normal interest in food and eating;
- consistent weight gain through early childhood, stable maintenance of weight in adolescence;
- eats regularly and moderately, consistent with activity level.

shows a relatively normal and stable level of activity.

THE CHILD IN TROUBLE:

shows some form of sleep disturbance—

- suddenly develops nightmares or other disturbances;
- develops insomnia (difficulty getting to sleep);
- shows *hypersomnia* (sleeping way too much);
- begins to show fitful, restless sleep or is "up and down" all night;
- fears going to sleep.

shows an appetite disturbance—

- sudden and dramatic changes in appetite;
- sudden and dramatic weight gain or loss;
- evidence of "binging and purging" (eating too much, then vomiting);
- evidence of anorexia (self-starvation; relentless pursuit of thinness);
- inappropriate interest in or distorted views of food and of eating.

shows dramatic escalation in activity level (hyperactivity), or sudden lethargy and fatigue.

Psychological Disruptions

When something is wrong children will often show the effects of the stress or trauma through alterations in their psychological or emotional life. Again, since children tend to show a certain amount of day-to-day variability, it's important to attune to a *pattern* of changes.

The Child You Know:
is pretty much on a developmentally appropriate level of functioning—
- age-appropriate interests and maturity level;
- shows a steadily progressive pattern of development;
- shows a wide range of coping abilities;
- deals with stress well enough for his or her age;
- responds to discipline in a predictable manner;
- shows appropriate responses to different situations;
- can contain emotions in a healthy, stable manner.

The Child in Trouble:
shows dramatic changes in developmental functioning—
- shows *regressive* behaviors (behaviors that were normal at earlier ages, but are inappropriate for the present age), such as "baby talk," thumb-sucking, preoccupation with toys or objects popular at an earlier age;
- shows repetitive or *driven* behaviors, such as hair pulling, tugging at genitalia, tics, or any other behavior that might be dismissed as simply "nervous habits" by a parent less knowledgeable than you;

GUIDELINES FOR DEALING WITH
PEDIATRICIANS (PART II)
BY VITO A. PERRIELLO, M.D.

The major philosophy behind pediatrics is advocacy for children. With that in mind, the pediatrician has the child's well-being, health, and protection as the top priorities. Obviously, the family unit, whatever form that might take, is an integral part of the child's world. You should keep that in mind when approaching the pediatrician.

IF YOU LIVE IN THE SAME TOWN OR AREA AS YOUR CHILD:

- Get to know your child's pediatrician.
- Take your child to the doctor on your watch when necessary.
- Provide copies of any court documents that will help the pediatrician be able to release information to you and provide you with the information you need.
- Understand insurance coverage and payment arrangements in advance—don't let your child get caught in the middle of a tug-of-war over physician reimbursement.
- Work with your pediatrician to facilitate the transfer of medicine, instructions for treatments, required follow-ups, etc., when you transfer your child.
- If differences of opinion and/or philosophies exist over specific parenting or health issues, such as discipline, eating, immunizations, etc., use the pediatrician as a mediator and educator.
- Recognizing that lifestyles are different, it is still advisable for youngsters to have similar schedules in each household, especially if school days and homework are involved.

IF YOU LIVE IN ANOTHER TOWN OR COMMUNITY:

- find a local pediatrician and establish a relationship with him or her. Obtain a referral from friends, neighbors, the local community hospital or the local medical society.
- make contact with the office, bring them your "papers," explain your situation, and find out what types of information the pediatrician needs.
- obtain copies of your child's medical records from his or her "home" pediatrician and provide them to your local doctor. Documents such as immunization records, allergies to medicines and foods, and any other significant health issues are particularly important.
- always obtain records of your office visits and provide them to your ex or to your child's local pediatrician.
- if there seem to be contradictory approaches or advice between the two physicians, do whatever you can to help them talk to each other to resolve these issues.

- shows ritualistic behaviors: behaviors that must be performed in a rigid, ritualistic manner, with a catastrophic reaction if the behavior is interrupted;
- shows sudden fascination or preoccupation with violence, weapons, aggressive and/or sadistic material, etc.;
- shows sudden onset of phobias (unrealistic fears of typically benign objects or situations);
- shows sudden onset of physical complaints *in the absence of any medical problem*, sudden over-concern with body parts or functions;

- shows sudden onset of mood swings, eruptions of anger, and so on.

DISTURBANCES IN SOCIAL FUNCTIONING

As your child grows older, you have less of an opportunity to observe his functioning in the greater community. But if you're attentive and know what to look for, you will also pick up on changes in his social adaptation.

THE CHILD YOU KNOW:
is an active, enthusiastic participant in activities, both in the home and in the community, with a wide range of healthy relationships with other children and adults alike—

- shows solid friendships, which last through the normal "ups and downs" of normal relationships;
- develops friendships with children who share similar values and mores;
- is enthusiastic about having you get to know her friends and like them, and having them like you as well;
- enjoys healthy, growth-promoting activities;
- identifies with a group or several groups with shared interests and goals;
- participates in community activities, such as scouts, church or synagogue involvement, volunteer groups, organized sports, or something else;
- is generally "engaged" with the family and participates in the flow of family activities.

THE CHILD IN TROUBLE:
shows dramatic changes in her functioning both within the
home and the community—

- rapid, chaotic changing of friendships;
- excessive devaluing of other youngsters;
- the classic "wrong crowd" scenario;
- isolation from family members, withdrawal from family
  activities;
- increase in secretive types of behaviors;
- loss of interest in things that used to be fun or enjoyable,
  particularly if these things are now devalued;
- dropping out of activities that are healthy and growth-
  promoting;
- behavioral difficulties at school;
- marked decrease in school performance, grades, effort;
- disrespect toward other adults in the community.

BEHAVIORAL DISTURBANCES

These are pretty easy to spot, and certain of the behaviors listed
below are most definitely "red flags" or definite danger signals.

THE CHILD YOU KNOW:
shows a flexible range of developmentally appropriate behaviors—

- respect for the property and physical integrity of others;
- a caretaking attitude toward animals;
- a fundamental sense of "fair play";
- appropriate control of sexual and aggressive impulses;
- respect for his or her own body integrity and hygiene;

- interest in active, social, and "healthy" pursuits;
- participation in organized activities requiring cooperation.

THE CHILD IN TROUBLE:

shows anti-social or self-destructive patterns of behavior—

- sudden loss of interest in hygiene;
- shoplifting, stealing both at home and in the community;
- loss of interest in activities formerly pleasurable;
- cruelty to animals;
- fire-setting;
- aggression against others, disregard for their safety;
- self-mutilating behaviors (not just piercings or tattoos, although we discourage these, too; we're talking about cutting on the inner thighs or wrists or otherwise mutilating the flesh);
- vandalism, destruction of property;
- sexual acting out, particularly with younger or defenseless children;
- drug and/or alcohol abuse.

Most of these behaviors warrant immediate attention, particularly if the child engages in them alone. Sometimes groups of children will get "carried away" and a child will do things that he or she would never think of doing alone. These behaviors undertaken alone are much more disturbing than acting out in the group context.

FALSE ACCUSATIONS OF ABUSE

Ugh. This is such a distasteful topic. The stories we could tell you. They would curl every hair on your head, if you have any left. But we won't. We put this topic off as long as we could, but it has to be dealt with. Because it does happen. Based on our experience, it could very well happen to you. There is no way to inoculate yourself against false accusations of abuse, either physical or sexual. There are no safeguards that you can put into place to guarantee that this won't happen to you.

There are few things that can be so damaging to a man. It creates a lasting cloud of doubt over everything you will ever do as a parent from that moment on. It is impossible to prove that you *didn't* do something. You will never be completely exonerated. Your best hope is to benefit from the fact that there is "insufficient evidence" to prove that you did. You can hear the ring of suspicion in that phrase, *"insufficient evidence."*

If such an accusation is lodged against you, there is also not much we can offer you, except for sympathy and a little advice. An accusation of abuse is not just an accusation of a specific act. It's also a statement about your mental health—about the way you relate to others—and, most importantly, about your ability to control yourself. The last thing you want to do is to respond in a way that makes you *look* irrational and unstable. If you have been falsely accused, our best advice to you is to hold your head up high, respond with strength and dignity, and, most of all, get yourself a good lawyer. A really good lawyer. Fight these false allegations decisively and to the full extent of your ability. But let your attorney pound the table. Let your attorney rant and rave. Give absolutely no credence to the allegations by letting your emotions get the best of you.

As for your kids—especially the one in the center of this mess—no matter what the situation, this has to be confusing at best and traumatic at worst for her. No matter what the situation, the bottom line is that this is a profound sadness. Your job at this point is to do everything you can to make her feel safe and secure. Even if this means not seeing her for a while. Even if this means "supervised" visitation for a period of time. Try to make the time that you do have with her and the others as normal as possible. You don't need to prove your innocence to her. She knows. You don't have to prove that your ex has done a cruel, terrible thing. This won't help her. You simply have to ride this out, heed the advice of your attorney and other helpful folks, and try to keep damage to a minimum.

As for your ex, the only way we can help you is for you to get some perspective on what she's done. No doubt, this act stemmed from a wish for you to "disappear" from her life and from the lives of your children. To simply go away and cease to exist. But you won't go away, and you won't do anything to jeopardize your relationship with your children. You will stay and fight. For as long as it takes. She can't erase you from the picture.

An accusation designed to get rid of you must backfire, because now you're more committed than ever to remaining in your child's life. You're in it for the long haul, especially now, because you realize that for your ex to commit such a damaging, primitive act means she hasn't mourned. The cruelty of the act shows just how much she hasn't mourned. When you realize this, you must approach this situation with sadness, not rage—with dignity and strength, not vengeance—and with the goal of protecting your children, rather than destroying your ex. Your child will benefit in the end.

AN OUNCE OF PREVENTION . . .

Assuming you have not been accused of any type of abuse, we can offer here some ways to protect yourself, to prevent even the remotest *hint* of any behavior that someone with evil intent could use against you. We've discussed the things that women seem to know intuitively that just escape the male brain. We've discussed safety issues, both in the home and in the neighborhood, and we've offered some straight talk about other important things. In discussing protecting yourself and your kids, we turned to our friend, pediatrician Dr. Raymond Ford, for advice. We discussed our interests in this area with him and asked for his input, and he called us shortly thereafter to tell us that he had "jotted down some thoughts" for us. We could not possibly improve on his own words, so we will present them to you just as he wrote them to us:

Dear Dan and Jerry,

As you have probably mentioned in your book, men don't ask for directions. Nowhere is this more evident than in the doctor's office. The issue seems to be one of raw vulnerability and the fear of our ignorance being exposed. An example or two:

Fathers are often unaware of, or selectively stupid about, female hygienic needs. This can lead to problems if the child is a four-year-old girl who hasn't the slightest notion that her failure to wipe "in the right direction" may cause vaginal irritation, urinary tract infection, or (worse for you) the appearance of abuse. There are techniques for female bathing which are secrets known only to them. Ask your ex-spouse about them—she'll love your humility. Or, if need be, your mother, your sister, your wife, or new girlfriend. Even doctors can help. This is an authentic area of vulnerability for fathers. Admit it.

Another situation that may arise is one of women's hair styling. We have seen little girls in the office who appear to be neglected and uncared-for simply because Dad didn't have the slightest notion about how hair is supposed to lie on a girl's head. The difference between looking like a ragamuffin and like a well-tended little girl can rest upon something as simple as hair care. Learn how to part and put up her hair and how to use the little gadgets that hold it all together, like barrettes and, heaven forbid, ribbons. The message is this: Don't, through your innocent ignorance, appear to be neglectful.

Of a more serious nature was a recent situation in which a child was catastrophically mauled by a pit bull. The little boy was visiting with his mother in a strange home—the family home of her new boyfriend. The boy wandered too near the unrestrained dog and was nearly killed. You have a responsibility here, also. The mother was simply unaware that guard dogs are likely to attack a child in that situation. Talk together about safety in the homes into which your child will now venture. Discuss it **before** the accident. Are there guard dogs (specifically pit bulls, Rottweilers, Dobermans)? Are there likely to be loaded guns or alcoholic beverages accessible? Matches or cigarette lighters? Swimming pools or ponds? We once had a little patient who wandered off and nearly drowned in the farm pond of his stepfather's family. Simply because no one thought to take precautions necessary for a young child. Specifically, discuss home safety with your pediatrician, and especially with your ex, your new partner, and anyone else who may be involved in the care of your child.

Know which bruises matter and which are but the marks left by normal childhood's exuberance. So much is mentioned about protecting yourself from accusations of abuse and neglect, but you also will continue to ensure your child's safety as she is cared for by new "others." Significant buttock bruising, large or unusually shaped torso bruises, and those on the cheeks might arouse suspicion. Quarter-sized forehead bruises and bumps, as well as those on the front of the lower legs are almost always "normal." Consult with your pediatrician. Most often this will help, as unnecessary confrontation with your ex can be avoided.

There are a number of problems caused by pure ignorance. Be on the lookout for them, for emotional crises may follow and be difficult to unravel. Bed-wetting is a classic example of this. Many normal children are bed-wetters, particularly little boys. If you are living with a new significant other, be certain that she knows that your child is not to blame, nor can he control this condition. We have had patients for whom this became a major focus of family discontent. Other examples are "habit tics," obesity or chronic overeating, asthma, and attention deficit disorder. Ask your pediatrician for literature on these *conditions, and handle them medically, and not as though they are a by-product of the conflict in the child's life.*

Sincerely,

Ray

As you can see, this issue is no different from any other that we have discussed throughout the course of this book. Learn as much as you can. Don't be afraid to own up to what you don't know. Don't be afraid to "ask for directions." Use the resources around you. Most of all, use your head. Get into a mindset of protection and safety for your children, even though they're not with you all the time—*especially* because they're not with you all the time. Manage your end of things responsibly and with care. Apply your experience and common sense in all areas of managing your children. Be fun without being reckless. Be cautious without being a ninny. Be protective without being overanxious. And be vigilant without being paranoid.

FOR THE DAD WITH A NEW FAMILY

"SOMETIMES I FEEL LIKE AN ORPHAN"

Jason is 10. He's a handsome kid, possessed of an easy smile and winsome demeanor. He's really bright, but sort of a mediocre student. He's a baseball player, pretty good glove, but no stick, and he wants a go-kart just about more than anything else in this world. He enjoys a wide range of friendships, and girls think he's cute. And he is. But he's also depressed. He feels sad and lonely. The first thing he said when he walked through McClure's door was "I feel like I'm an orphan."

Jason has two parents who care a great deal about him. They've been divorced for about five years. They have shared custody, 50-50, and they have managed this situation well. And Jason did well. He adjusted to his mother's remarriage, and he even likes her new husband. He adjusted to his dad's remarriage, although dad's new wife took some getting used to.

So why is he depressed? Well, in the course of just 18 months his mother and stepfather had a baby, and so did his father and stepmother. They did all the right things. They included him in all the planning, in decorating the nursery, in all the shopping for newborn stuff, and everything else. And they shared their excitement with him, talking about being a "big brother" and all. And he was excited, too . . . sort of.

But then came the births, first a girl to his mother and step-father and then a boy to his father and stepmother. And all of a sudden he had a "brother" and a "sister." And as each respective parental unit began to dote on the newborn child, in much the same way that each parent had doted on Jason, he began to experience an awkward, sinking feeling. The feeling that he really didn't have a true family. That he was part of a "new" family on each side. And all of a sudden he began to feel sort of like an outsider. Like he was just a "visitor," no matter where he went. And he began to feel very much alone.

"THEY'RE LIVING MY LIFE"

Susan is 12, and into all of the things 12-year-old girls are into. She was only seven when her mom left her dad and moved into an apartment. For almost six years she has lived with her mother and "visited" her dad in her former house. Things worked out fairly well. She was able to adjust to apartment living with her mother, and still had the comfort of her old bedroom when she "visited" with her father. He kept all of her posters on the wall, and she still had her stuffed animal collection spread all over the bed (so that even if she didn't make up her bed, you couldn't tell because of all the animals). And things worked out well, because her mom moved to an apartment in the school district, and Susan could keep all of her friends, even if her parents were divorced and living apart.

But then Susan's dad started "seeing" someone. Someone who had three children—and one of them was in Susan's grade at school. Over the Christmas break her dad married this woman, and she and her three children moved into dad's house. The 12-year-old moved into Susan's room—and kept all her posters on the wall, adding some of her own. She put all of the stuffed animals in the closet, putting her own on the bed. Susan's dad talked to her a lot about this, about the changes that would take place, and how he was convinced that Susan would adjust okay. Dad thought this would actually be kind of cool for Susan, because she would have a "ready-made" playmate in the home whenever she came for visitation.

Well, Susan didn't think it was "cool." She was devastated. On the first visit she was only there for 45 minutes before she called her mom to come and get her. She hated the fact that her dad had remarried. She hated the fact that her dad's "new daughter" was a classmate. Most of all, she hated the fact that this girl was living with *her* dad, sleeping in *her* room, with *her* stuff all around. Living *her* life. And she didn't think this was fair.

It's Not The "What," It's The "How"

We couldn't begin to offer you complete prescriptions for navigating the stormy seas of the "blended family," with all of its combinations and permutations. We're sure entire books have been written on this topic, and we encourage you to seek them out. Our goal has been to help you see situations through the eyes of your child. We have also attempted to put forth the notion that often the *what* of a particular situation isn't nearly as important as the *how*. So, it's not so important *that* you remarry, it's *how* you remarry. It's not so important *that* you may have stepchildren living with you, it's *how* you integrate these children into the lives of your children. It's not so important *that* your ex remarries, it's *how* you handle her remarriage. This is no time for you to be selfish. Your kids are going to need your help.

In this vein, we'd like to offer a few Indisputable Truths.

Indisputable Truth #1
Emotions Are Weird

Let's face it, lots of times emotions just don't make sense. This may be especially true of children who have experienced trauma or significant upset, and it may be intensified if they were unable to exert any control over their situation. And especially if they have been unable to express, or at times even acknowledge, the depth or breadth of their emotional response. The emotions experienced by children whose parents divorce are deeply felt, and typically children are poorly equipped to articulate, understand, and fully work through these feelings. They will variously experience:

- **sadness** and a profound sense of loss—their lives have changed unalterably;
- **fear** that nothing is permanent—that he will be the one to be rejected;
- **confusion** over conflicting loyalties and feelings;
- **anxiety** over conflicts that seemingly can't be resolved;
- **guilt** that she may have been at fault or contributed to the divorce;
- **rage** over being "jerked around";
- **envy** of your relationship with new Significant Others;
- **jealousy** that others will possess what is "rightfully" his;
- **disloyalty** because she's becoming attached to people who dislike each other.

These emotions can crop up at any time, with little provocation. They often will conflict with one another. They don't always make sense; in fact, they *seldom* make sense. But they're there, they are apt to be intense, and, if you're in the process of blending a family, you're about to provoke them.

When you, as a father, see these emotions erupt in your child, you see that they hurt. You feel their impact on your child and perhaps even on yourself. You feel the pressure to *do something* about them. To make them all better; to make them go away; to convince your child that they're not really there; to simply deny their existence altogether. But you must resist, because "doing something" doesn't get the job done.

The best thing you can do for your child is to simply tolerate these emotions. Don't be afraid of them. Don't react to them impulsively. Don't try to *do* anything about them. Allow them to emerge, tolerate them, and help your youngster understand that they're a normal part of the process. Even if they're weird and don't particularly make sense. They're there, and nothing can change that. They simply have to be "aired out" and worked through over time. This is not to say you have to tolerate every behavioral *expression* of these feelings, because you don't. In fact, it's your job as a father to help your youngster find appropriate modes of expression. But you have to accept the feelings.

Indisputable Truth #2
Your Kid's View of Things Differs from Yours

In our clinical experience with the blending of families, there are few situations where the perceptions of the parent are so at odds with the perceptions of the child. You'd be amazed at how often a parent will come in all starry-eyed, enthusiastic, and optimistic, convinced that the child shares their enthusiasm and excitement. Then the kid comes in despondent, frustrated, and with a "doomsday" scenario.

You've mourned the loss of your marriage. You've dealt with it emotionally. And you've found someone whom you believe can make you happy. You also might just be a little desperate to "move on." But don't assume that your child feels the same way. You've been emotionally preparing for this for a while. She hasn't. You've been looking for a new relationship. She hasn't. You see great personal gain in "moving on." She doesn't. You're in love, excited, and enthusiastic. She isn't. But most importantly, you come to this situation from the perspective of a mature adult. She doesn't.

You need to acknowledge these differences to be able to help her through this. You can help her a great deal if you just talk to her about these things. Don't try to protect your excitement and enthusiasm by denying her the opportunity to be heard. Don't allow yourself to deny that she has strong feelings that are quite different from yours. Listen to her. Let her air her feelings. You don't have to *do* anything. Your job is not to talk her out of them, or change her mind, or make these feelings go away. You simply need to let her talk about them.

INDISPUTABLE TRUTH #3
THE SENSE OF LOSS IS REAL, POWERFUL, AND ALWAYS PRESENT

Your child has lost a great deal. He lost his parents' marriage. He's likely lost some of his innocence, some of his childhood. He's lost some of his sense of security. He's lost seeing his parents in a loving relationship. And most importantly, he's lost your full-time presence in the home. He couldn't avoid these losses, either. He wasn't calling the shots. He had to sit by and watch the changes happen. This sense of loss is hard to shake. It makes him much more sensitive to other potential losses. It makes him wary of change, especially when he's not the one in charge. It can make him fear change, even *good* change, because all change brings some measure of loss.

So, with this in mind, let's examine what you're asking of him, and try to view this through the prism of his sense of loss.

You're asking him to accept a decision that *you* have made. Even if you've asked for his input, you made the call. You're asking him to accept a major change in his life. You're asking him to accept new people into his life, and to accept them being a part of your life. You will help him a great deal if you are sensitive to the way he will experience these changes. Even if he can't control the situation, he will feel understood.

REUNION FANTASIES ARE REAL, POWERFUL, AND ALWAYS PRESENT

We mentioned this earlier. All children of divorce experience "reunion fantasies"—the deeply held wish that their parents would get back together. Sometimes this means a conviction that eventually the parents *will* get back together, and their bedrock sense of stability and security will be restored. Even when the marriage was lousy by any standard. Even though in reality you and your ex actually may be better off now. Even if your new love is great. It's just a fact of life.

These fantasies exist, and they don't die easily. We've dealt with numbers of youngsters who, even after both parents have remarried and had children of their own, continued to harbor a wish, at times even a conviction, that their parents will reunite. Obviously, it takes a lot of denial to hold on to these fantasies.

Your new significant other threatens this denial. She introduces the possibility that the divorce is final, which may be just too much reality for the denial system to withstand. Your child is apt to have quite a strong reaction, and, if you don't understand where the reaction is coming from, you can really do some harm. To avoid doing harm, you must avoid the tendency to take this personally. You must avoid the tendency to see these behaviors as motivated by more mature aims. Otherwise you'll be inclined to attack, which will be devastating. Unfortunately, your best position is simply to understand, to be generally sympathetic, and to just "ride it out" as these issues come to some resolution.

INDISPUTABLE TRUTH #5
LOYALTY CONFLICTS ARE REAL, POWERFUL, AND ALWAYS PRESENT

If you stop to think about it, you really are asking a lot of your youngster when you introduce a new Significant Other into his life. Even though they aren't always able to articulate it, children are remarkably loyal creatures. As we discussed earlier, they're predisposed to think that their parents (warts and all) are simply the greatest. This is normal, healthy, and it promotes their sense of well-being. This makes it hard for them to become attached to another adult without real conflict and ambivalence—even if the other adult is sensitive, kind, loving, and an all-around great person. In fact, sometimes these qualities even make it worse. He sees your new love under what are likely the best of circumstances, while he has probably seen his mom under conditions of great stress and conflict.

So, expect a lot of behaviors that don't make sense. Expect him to be warm and cuddly toward her one minute, only to turn on her the next. Expect to overhear him telling his friends how great she is, only to have him turn around and tell you he hates her. Expect him to excitedly ask if she's going to be there when you pick him up, only to have him snub her when you arrive.

You must understand that these behaviors don't necessarily make sense to him, either. He may not understand that the closer he gets to your new love, the more his attachment to his mother seems threatened. He's not yet able to understand that you can become attached to one person without it affecting your attachment to another. Again, your job is not to solve his dilemma for him. Your job is to simply understand, tolerate, and be there for him in spite of everything.

INDISPUTABLE TRUTH #6

Your Gain May Well Be Her Loss

If you have a new love, odds are you're experiencing that "high" that comes with all new relationships, and it feels good. If your divorce (and marriage) was horrible, this is an especially welcome relief to you. You're excited. You have something to look forward to for a change. You have a renewed sense of purpose and belonging. This is good. And healthy.

But, however good this is for you, your daughter may not share this newfound excitement. Quite the contrary, your enthusiasm may serve only to heighten her sense of loss. Or betrayal. So think about it. What would you do if you were in her situation? Would you welcome this interloper with open arms? Would you suppress your own feelings of loss and rage, just because you know how happy your dad is? Would you realize that, in the long run, your dad's happiness is very important to your ultimate well-being, and simply keep your mouth shut? Would you really buy that line that "three parents are better than two"?

Of course not. You'd be immature, self-centered, and ego-centric. You'd be furious, and maybe just a little scared. And you would:

- pout;
- do everything in your power to make the grown-ups feel as bad as you do;
- say things like "She's not my mother! She can't tell me what to do!";
- feel jealous, rejected, and cast aside;
- —you can fill in the blank.

There's only so much of you to go around, you know. Every new person you introduce into your life will compete with her for your time, your attention, and your love. Your sensitivity and understanding of this fact will be central to her ability to adjust.

INDISPUTABLE TRUTH #7

As Always, Your Job Is to Keep Your Eyes on the Prize

These changes are apt to bring up many conflicting emotions on your part as well. You're embarking on a new lifestyle, with new responsibilities and many uncertainties. And in spite of your enthusiasm and excitement, you will also have nagging fears, anxieties, and insecurities. You may also feel under pressure, under the gun to "make this one work." You're taking on an entire set of new demands, with more people competing for your time. You may worry over spreading yourself too thin.

Your job is to do as we have encouraged you to do all along. Be strong. Be confident. Take care of yourself without being selfish. Be decisive without being dictatorial. Help your child to tolerate emotional upheaval by managing your own emotions appropriately. Resist the temptation to *act* on your child's emotions. Learn to tolerate and accept, while helping them to express their emotions in healthy ways. Don't rush, be patient. Time is on your side, and while time doesn't heal *all* wounds, it will certainly heal some.

12

EYES ON THE PRIZE
Maintaining Perspective

You may be wondering if the authors of this book have ever experienced your anguish and concern. Have they ever experienced separation, divorce, custody battles, visitation? We have not. Our knowledge, our views, and our suggestions come from those who have trusted us to help them through their plight. We want you to know that the greatest lesson we've learned from our patients is respect. We have watched our patients play very tough hands, and play them well. Yes, they've suffered deep pain, anger, and self-doubt. But we've also seen impressive displays of restraint, sensitivity, and dignity in the face of inordinately stressful situations.

We have learned that divorced men can teach us a lot about restoring broken relationships. They can be wonderful fathers to their children. They can also be exceptional husbands, under better circumstances. We wrote this book, in great part, as a tribute to these men. And as a tribute to you. No matter how you may have reacted in the past, you can join the ranks of men who have become powerful influences in their children's lives—men who have, despite their own grief and pain, saved their children from many of the potential scars of divorce. If we didn't believe in you, we never would have written this book.

TRANSCENDING THE MOMENT

One of the biggest mistakes you can make as a noncustodial father is to allow your relationship to your children to be defined by "visitation." If you define the relationship just in terms of the time you actually spend with them, you'll only be cheating yourself.

A father's relationship to his children spans much more than the time they spend together. Think of all the men who have to be away from their children for significant periods of time. Military men. Men who must travel in their jobs. Men who must be out of town much of the week for work. How do you suppose these guys manage to have good relationships with their kids? Perhaps they would be role models for you to investigate.

The most successful fathers we know are not necessarily the ones who have the most time with their children. They are the ones who use their creativity, their resources, and their ingenuity to establish relationships with their kids that *transcend the moment* of visitation, the inevitably limited amount of time they spend together.

Even though you have to say goodbye to your kids more than you would wish, this doesn't mean that the experiences you share end at your ex's driveway. If you can find areas of common interest with your kids, you will find things that will bond them to you, even during your absences. These interests will increase your child's anticipation of time spent with you. They are things he will do in the intervening time to share with you when he sees you again—things she'll think about during the rest of the week, and share with you next time. Things that help her carry a part of you with her when she gets out of the car.

FIND YOUR CONSULTANTS

If you're in the dark about what to do, think how you would proceed in other circumstances. What would you do if your business was about to enter a previously unknown venture? What would you do if you needed to make a big new purchase, but were unfamiliar with the product? What would you do if you had to undertake any unfamiliar task? You would learn as much as you could, and you would take advantage of the experts in that area.

Your consultants for transcending the moment include other dads. Look for fathers who seem to have successful relationships with their children. Learn what they do to build beyond the moments spent together. Don't copy them necessarily; emulate their creativity and ingenuity. Check out hobby shop and craft store owners. They have an endless supply of ideas for hobbies, collections, avocations, and projects. They love this stuff, and their enthusiasm can be infectious. Then there are the leaders of organized activities, from scouts to sports. Participating in organized activities with your child is a great way to share common interests. A word of caution, though. These activities can become demanding and time-intensive, and therefore should only be initiated with the consent and cooperation of your ex. Otherwise, it may end up doing more harm than good.

As with anything else, the activity itself is not that important. What is important, however, is the gusto with which you approach the activity. The goal is not the end product. The goal is to transcend the moment. Don't ever forget it.

A FEW CHAMPS

Our hats are off to a number of dads we've known who have crafted areas of interest to share with their kids, solely out of their own creativity, enthusiasm, and ingenuity. And their kids loved it.

MR. BROKER: This fellow had a son who was seriously into money. When his son was young, he provided him with a regular "allowance" to be used to buy stocks. Together they researched certain stocks, decided on the best options for their interests, and the boy made the purchase. They transcended the moment by following the stock market on a daily basis watching these stocks. Each knew that every morning they were doing the same thing, reading the same stock quotes. When it came time to sell, the profits went to the boy's account to be used for future purchases. Not only did this kid learn a lot about managing money, but he and his dad had a very real and unbreakable common bond. His son is a grown man now, and they still do it.

MR. HORTICULTURIST: This dad converted his interest in gardening to a transcendent exercise. His daughter shared his interest, and together they developed a number of ongoing gardening projects. They developed an indoor garden under glass, a terrarium, for the winter months. They learned how to germinate their own seeds indoors as something they could do while they were waiting for the weather to get warm enough for planting. She charted the development of these seeds through germination, and eventually developed hybrids on her own. They each had an outdoor plot of their own and a common plot which they planned out together. They grew all manner of flowers and vegetables, and even when she was a teenager and had a host of outside interests, she continued to find time—her *own* time!—to swing by her dad's house and tend to her plots.

Mr. Bookie: This fellow shared a common interest in sports with his son, particularly baseball. Together they played "rotisserie baseball" way before it became institutionalized. They picked two players from each position to create their own All-Star team and had a wager on which would be superior at the end of the year. They also wagered a pack of baseball cards on which team would be in first, and which would be in the cellar, at various points in the season. Again, every day each would race to the morning paper, no matter whose house the boy was in, and read stats from the night before. There were frenzied telephone calls some weeknights and Saturday afternoons either to gloat or to commiserate. But they won, no matter what the outcome of their wagers, because they transcended the moment.

Mr. "I Have a Cause": We've also known a number of dads who have brought their children into their social/political activism— as far as we know, without unduly pushing their ideas onto the kids. Working together on environmental issues, animal welfare projects, community service projects, etc., can all be exemplary ways to transcend the moment.

WEDNESDAY EVENINGS ....

New Opportunities

You have a lot of advantages over fathers of the past when it comes to constructing a relationship with your child that transcends artificial constraints of "visitation."

First and foremost, if you're fortunate enough to have access to computers, you have the incomparable luxury of e-mail. E-mail allows you to communicate with your child without having to use the telephone. Your ex controls the other end of the phone line, for starters, and it really would be obnoxious for you to be calling her home all the time. Plus, kids aren't always great telephone conversationalists. Surely you've seen your daughter on the phone with her mother, and you see her nod her head or even just shrug in response to a question. Even though they may be able to talk on the phone for hours with friends, their conversations with you, or any other adult, for that matter, are typically brief, terse, and goal-directed.

E-mail avoids all of these pitfalls. Your child can receive and send messages at his leisure, on his time. He doesn't have to be interrupted. He doesn't have to search for ways to fill the silences. And he doesn't have to communicate with you while someone else may possibly be listening to his end of the conversation. You can use e-mail to send your kid information that you've found, updates on your projects, and all other kinds of stuff, even if you're on different coasts. Use it. If you don't have it, get it if at all possible. It's a tremendous asset to your relationship.

Second, you're in a good position now, culturally. There is an increasing trend toward more support and more resources for fathers in their efforts to build positive relationships with their children. You're limited only by your creativity, your enthusiasm, your ingenuity, and your drive to have the best possible relationship with your kids.

THE PRIZE (AND KEEPING YOUR EYES ON IT)

Now we'd like to shift gears. Until now we've concentrated on a more or less "nuts and bolts" approach to the important issues facing you as you raise your children. Now we're going to wax philosophical. After all, we've got tons of money invested in all our advanced degrees, and, if our mothers ever read this book, we want them to be assured that this was money well spent. Anyway, we can only be specific and down-to-earth for so long.

Our experience has been that people can benefit a great deal from pointed "how-to" recommendations. But it's also important to be able to connect "*what*" with "*why*." Especially when times get tough, it's important that you understand why you're doing things in a particular way or coming at the situation from a certain angle. Otherwise, you have a tendency to revert to old, unsuccessful patterns of behavior.

In this section we hope to address some of the philosophical issues we have found to be important not only in our practices, but also in parenting our own children.

DELUSIONS OF OWNERSHIP AND TIMELESSNESS

On the occasion of the wedding of Saffer's younger daughter, he was invited to address the group that had gathered to celebrate the event. While collecting his thoughts in anticipation of his talk, he came to realize that this was really a bittersweet moment. A happy occasion, to be sure, but also one that brings a measure of sadness. Especially to a father.

As father of the bride, one of his tasks was to "give the bride away" to her new husband. It dawned on him that for her entire life he had held on to a belief that was merely an illusion—the belief that she had actually *belonged* to him. As he pondered the fact that her marriage was actually a new beginning for her, with her entire life ahead of her, it also dawned on him that he had operated under an illusion of timelessness.

The burden of parenting is awesome. Your children are always in your thoughts, whether or not you're aware of it consciously. They require tremendous time and energy, and it's a never-ending task. When you're caught up in the day-to-day grind of work, parenting, disciplining, worrying, yelling, laughing, and shouldering the awesome burden of fatherhood, there's a tendency to see life through a very narrow lens.

You develop the sense that these beings *belong* to you. You're responsible for making them people—functional, decent, and good people. People who can be polite but assertive, ambitious but caring, competitive but sportsmanlike, organized but not rigid, playful but not irresponsible. The list goes on and on and on. Though it may not always seem so, you have a great deal of power and control over them, and they depend and rely on you for so many things.

Even when they develop friendships and activities outside the home, you continue to believe that you own them. Your sense of ownership is sustained even through the teen years, when their attitudes and attachments change, when they assert their own individuality and autonomy and they may even have little use for you. Sometimes your investment of time, energy, and protectiveness is so great that the sense of ownership actually increases.

But the ownership is just a delusion. It's a particularly painful one for a man in your circumstance. To make matters worse, divorce proceedings and custody battles only serve to accentuate this delusion of ownership. Battles over custody and visitation are framed in the context of who "possesses" the children, as if ownership is at stake.

In fact, neither you nor your ex "owns" your children. They're just on loan for a few years. Then they own themselves. Your job is to help them to own themselves responsibly. To do this, you must accept the fact that you *don't* own them.

If you cling to the delusion of ownership, you'll feel threatened when they assert their individuality. You'll be angry when they behave in ways that are not consistent with what you would prescribe for them. When you should be celebrating their strides toward independence, you'll be feeling a sense of personal loss and despondency instead. When they fall in love you'll be hurt rather than joyful. When they leave, you'll feel like you've "lost" them. But you can't lose them if you didn't own them. Your time, energy, effort, tears, and laughter are not reflections of ownership. They are investments of love, investments in the future. You are their father, and always will be.

Which brings us to the second delusion, that of timelessness. Again, in the daily grind of work, parenting, and all of the other things you do, there's a natural tendency to lose sight of the big picture. Often we're so busy taking care of our responsibilities that we don't realize how quickly time passes. We tend to hold the delusion that our children will always be children. And will always need us. No such luck.

You have very few years to actually parent your children. This time is especially precious when access to your kids is limited. You need to decide how you're going to use this time. Are you going to let this time be eaten away by conflict, stress, anger, and continued struggles with your ex? Or will you be able to put these issues behind you and use this time to actively parent your child?

This time is a gift. You can't control how much you've been given. It can't be created and you can't borrow more if you misuse what you have. You can't return it or buy more of it once you've wasted it. If it passed you by because you were angry, gloomy, or otherwise preoccupied, you can't get a refund.

But you *can* extend time if you play your cards right. Just as time wasted in self-pity, anger, or gloom becomes self-limiting, time spent in joyful activities with your children has a way of expanding and multiplying itself. Joyful activity not only gives pleasure, it also makes us want it to last longer. We want to seek it out at every opportunity.

Time spent in preoccupation will drive your children into themselves, even when they're with you. Who wants to be with a guy who is always sad, resentful, or angry? Joyful time will make them want to really *be* with you when they're with you. It will allow them to truly get to know you and to carry you with them even when you're apart. Time wasted in preoccupation, hostility, or gloom will drive them to seek solace elsewhere. Joyful time will draw them to you.

Joyful time doesn't have to be all fun and games. Anybody can do fun stuff with kids, that's no challenge. It's the hard stuff that makes you "Dad." Even discipline, correction, and arguing can be joyful, if done with love and if tempered with mercy and compassion—and if you keep things in perspective and keep your eyes on the prize. Even though they're not always pleasant at the moment, they're the things that make you a father, that make you a special person in your child's life. That's joy.

GRIEF AND PETTINESS: THEY ROB THE SOUL

DISCLAIMER: The individuals discussed below are completely fictional. The situations and circumstances, however, are derived from actual clinical material from our practices. Any resemblance to real people, living or deceased, is purely coincidental. Any resemblance to YOU, however, should cause you great concern and send you running to your nearest shrink.

GRIEF

Brooke is 16. She's a beautiful girl, popular and well liked by others. She's involved in a variety of activities at school, and while she's not a leader, she does assume positions of responsibility in her different clubs. She was not blessed with great intellect, and academics are not her strong suit. Her parents are concerned because she's begun to show signs of being sexually active, and her popularity among boys has recently skyrocketed. At the same time, however, she has become more and more distant from both parents, and teachers have voiced concerns that she's showing signs of depression.

Brooke's mother and father had an "amicable" divorce, meaning primarily that there was no bloodshed. Her parents simply "grew apart," and her mother, Alicia, no longer felt that the father was either willing or able to meet her needs. Her father, Bill, was pretty much absorbed in his own work, and tended to assume a rather passive stance throughout the end-stage of the marriage.

While they never fought when she was around, Brooke knew things weren't right. You could cut the tension with a knife. They never spoke to each other any more. She described it as like living in a rooming house, where the people are civil but uncomfortable with each other. She was almost relieved that night when they stood before her and said those six dreadful words: "Sit down, we have to talk . . . ."

She knew it was coming. She figured her dad would leave and get a place of his own, and she expected she would live with her mother and "visit" with her father. However, her mother got a job offer in a city some 60 miles away, which she had to accept to make it through the financial burden of the separation. Because she was so connected to her school and attached to her circle of friends, Brooke decided to remain in town with her father, seeing her mother most weekends and all summer.

Bill fell into a funk. Brooke said it was like living with Eeyore, the miserable, pessimistic donkey from *Winnie the Pooh*. When they were home together, he was often asleep or in the study working at the computer. At mealtimes he was morose. At first Brooke simply figured he missed her mother, and would get over it in time. And he did miss Alicia. He had sort of a bewildered, confused view of the separation, and didn't understand what he had done wrong. The separation left him feeling rejected and somehow "not good enough" for Alicia.

Brooke thought it would do him good to talk about it, and so she would encourage him to talk when they were together. But it didn't help, because it turned out this was all he could talk about. No discussing Brooke's interests, activities, or pursuits, like they used to do. Only lamentations about Alicia. No effort at joint interests or projects, unlike before. Only self-pitying talk about the marriage and endless musings on "what went wrong."

When she first came in for counseling, Brooke spoke of how she felt roles had been reversed: She felt she was being a parent and caretaker to her father, rather than the other way around. Bill had essentially made her his wife, as she assumed much the same role in the house that Alicia had filled in the marriage. This burden eventually caused her to distance herself from him and propelled her into sexual promiscuity.

Bill never got the message. He was so preoccupied with his own loss, sadness, and grief that he was unable to see what was happening before his very eyes.

PETTINESS

Wayne's two sons are eight and thirteen. They are fine young boys. Adam, the eight-year-old, is athletic, winsome, and wakes up each morning like this is going to be the greatest day of his life. Josh, the 13-year-old, is more reserved and docile. But he enjoys good friends, he's a whiz at computer games and analytic tasks, and he has a good head on his shoulders. These boys live with their mom, Martha, and see their father every other weekend and one evening per week. Wayne had a brief affair with a coworker, and Martha filed for divorce the moment she found out.

Martha, a professional, makes a pretty good living. She has dated casually, but has not remarried. Wayne lives in a town 15 miles away and is remarried. He and his wife have a child of their own, and they lead what might be described as a very stable, middle-class life. Martha and Wayne have worked hard to be solid parents, even though they can't stand one another. There has been no abuse, no alcoholism, no drug addiction, and no trauma in the lives of these children. The boys go to fine schools, and are well liked by both adults and peers. Josh is in psychotherapy for attempting to kill himself.

Why? Many reasons. But foremost is that this youngster feels that he is a chronic source of disappointment to his father, and will never be able to gain his approval.

You see, Wayne has never gotten over the fact that Martha no longer wanted to be married to him after the affair. He had always been in control and "called the shots," and even though he has remarried and gone on with his life, he cannot forgive Martha for kicking him out of the marriage. So he attacks. And he knows that her "weak spot" is her mothering ability, for she has always felt conflicted and a little guilty for being a working mother. His single-minded goal is to demonstrate to everyone, but particularly to the Court, her shortcomings as a mother. Unfortunately, the most direct route to this is through the product of her mothering, Josh. In his zeal to paint a picture of Martha as a bad mother, he must find fault with virtually everything about Josh.

Josh meanwhile is entering his teen years, and, well, you know how it is . . . . sometimes his person and his entire room just plain smells bad. Rather than help Josh learn how to keep his hygiene under control, Wayne cites this messiness as evidence of Martha's poor mothering. If Josh plays outside and gets dirty, it's no longer a normal sign of attending to "kid" things, it's evidence of laziness and a lack of self-discipline.

Rather than accept that part of Josh's natural makeup is to be sedentary rather than a jock, Wayne calls him a "couch potato." Wayne complains that Josh will simply turn into a blob of protoplasm because his mother doesn't make him jog three miles a day (which is what Wayne says he would do!). Rather than show an appreciation for Josh's analytic skills and computer expertise, Wayne calls him a nerd and laments that Josh will never be a "real man" because of the absence of a full-time role model (guess who).

When Josh is obedient, Wayne interprets it as passivity. When Josh cries, Wayne interprets it as weak and "feminine." When Josh plays group computer games that include girls, Wayne worries that other kids may think Josh is a sissy. When Josh shows a good appetite, Wayne interprets it as a lack of discipline in eating habits. When Josh tries to weasel our of homework, Wayne interprets it as a major character flaw.

Don't misunderstand. Wayne loves this kid. He really does. Although they're very different, he even *likes* Josh, and in many ways admires him. It's just that he cannot accept Josh as being "okay" because that would mean that Martha's parenting is okay. And you can't get custody of your kid if his mother is "okay."

You can't be your child's salvation, and the only one to mold him into the man you think he ought to be, if his mother is doing a good job. You can't "save" him from his mother if he's in good shape. Get the picture?

These are not "bad people." They are not evil. They are ordinary folks, just like you and me, trying to get by as best they can. But they have still done tremendous damage to their children. Bill became so preoccupied with his own grief and sadness that he was unable to provide Brooke with what she needed. He essentially surrendered his ability to "father" her. He put her in the position of having to "parent" him. Wayne, whose anger and narcissism drove him to pettiness in the extreme, very nearly sacrificed his son as a result.

When we say that grief and pettiness rob the soul, we're not talking about *your* soul, although God knows these things don't help you. You're grown, and you have to find ways to take care of your own soul. We appreciate the difficulty of your situation, but you cannot yield to grief, pettiness, or any of the other destructive emotions.

These things rob the souls *of your children*. By keeping them from getting your best. By preventing them from having enough constructive influence on their lives. By forcing them to surrender important aspects of their childhood—the only childhood they get.

It doesn't matter how angry you are. How sad you are. How guilty you are. How betrayed you are. What matters is that you do whatever you need to do in order to perform the job of FATHER.

ONE DAY AT A TIME

Alcoholics Anonymous has a saying . . . . actually, they have lots of little sayings. The one we happen to be interested in is "One Day at a Time." They appreciate the enormity of what they're up against, and they well know that in order to remain sober they must take life one day at a time. To do otherwise, to think about *never* having another drink, or *never* being able to enjoy oneself in a bar or at a cocktail party, is simply too much to handle. So they take life on, one day at a time.

You're facing a different kind of adversity, certainly. And unlike the alcoholic, you are not in complete control of your situation. But this "one day at a time" mentality applies to you just the same.

You can't dwell on the past, thinking how things *might have been* if only you had done one thing or another. The past is gone, and you did what you did. And so did she. And no matter how may regrets you have, how many "what if's" you can replay in your head, the past is gone. All you can do with it is to learn from it and hopefully avoid making similar mistakes in the future. But you can't change it and you need to get past it.

By the same token, you can't worry about the future and what it will bring. The future will bring what it brings. There's lots of water to go over the dam between now and the future. And the most important factor in what determines the future is what happens right now.

So . . .

Don't worry that he'll end up depressed—do what you can today to give him the tools he'll need for mental health.

Don't worry that she'll end up "just like her mother"—today, and every day, treat her as she is, for who she is.

Don't worry that you've harmed and damaged him—give him something in the here and now to hold on to.

Don't worry that you'll be ineffectual as a dad—read, listen, learn, and make yourself a good dad right now.

Don't worry that she'll be ruined by your wife's influence—give her the best possible role model she can have today.

Worry is just as evil and damaging as grief and pettiness. It accomplishes nothing. Actions accomplish things. Control what you can and leave the rest to fate. Have faith in yourself, and have a little faith in your kid. Do the right thing, and the odds are your kid will, too. Tolerate uncertainty, tolerate the lack of total control, and tolerate your anxiety, and you will arm your kid with a valuable model for dealing with stress. Succumb to your irresponsible or immature side, and you'll model that for him as well. Just take it one day at a time. Do what you can, don't worry about things that you can't control, and just do the best you can.

Tomorrow will take care of itself.

YOUR JOB DOESN'T STOP AT 18

This brings us to perhaps the most important message of the entire book. You're in this for the long haul. You will be your child's father forever. And nobody can take that away from you.

They can take your property. They can make claims against your income. They can even severely restrict your access to your child. But they can't do it forever. And they cannot alter the fact that you will be this child's father for all time.

That's why it's so important to keep your eyes on the prize. Your child will be old a lot longer than she'll be young. And being a father doesn't stop at 18. While the formative years are indeed crucial, these days it seems that many young people need their parents and families much more in the 18- to 24-year-old range than they do in the 14- to 18-year-old range. It's a tough world out there, and it takes an awful lot to make a go of it these days.

As young adults, they will not only need your support and love, they will also need your guidance. They will need the benefit of your experience. They will need the benefit of your maturity and your wisdom. They will need to know that you're there for them no matter what.

Your kids will be adults someday. They'll be able to make their own decisions, determine their own living arrangements, and decide for themselves how much contact they want with each parent. They'll be real people someday, and odds are they'll turn into people you like and admire. You will have years and years to relate to them as independent human beings in their own right. Without the burden of having to "parent" them. Without the burden of responsibility for their actions and behaviors. And without having to compete with your ex for time with them. Keep this in mind as you go through the day-to-day grind—it'll keep you sane. There's a lot of future at stake, so don't jeopardize it with pettiness now.

WEDNESDAY EVENINGS ....

These are the people who will carry your genes and your blood into the future. They will give you grandchildren. And your grandchildren will benefit from their experiences with you. These are the people who may well have to provide for *you*, God forbid, if something should happen to you. This is your family! *This* is what it's all about.

So don't screw it up now. Don't lose sight of the important in service of the immediate. Keep things in perspective. You may win a battle with your spouse and actually achieve that "victory" you so desperately want. But you may just poison the well in the process. Weigh every single thing you do against the prospect of crippling your future relationship with your child.

It doesn't seem like it in the throes of passion or anger, but there are many times when the best *long-range* strategy you can have is to let your ex win. In the short term it may hurt your pride, it may inconvenience you in some ways, and it may even not be particularly good for your child. In the short term. In the long run, however, you may gain by not spilling blood over it.

That's why it's so critical for you to maintain your dignity, your self-respect, and your perspective. These traits, not winning or losing the *conflict du jour,* will ultimately serve the best interests of your child. Because one day she will look back on this time with a mature perspective. She'll know who was acting like a baby and who wasn't. She'll know who was not playing by the rules and exploiting situations for their own gain. We hope she'll have a dad who can be proud of how he handled the situation. Not one who dragged his children through the muck.

He'll know someday that you really wanted to be there for *every single* birthday, Christmas, ball game, and school play. He'll understand someday why you weren't. Someday he'll understand the heartache you went through missing important parts of his growing up. But he'll also know how you would have done things if you could have. He will love you for it.

This is the ultimate payoff of parenthood, anyway. Kids who know that you love them, who know the sacrifices you've made, and who can look up to their dad. A dad they can be proud of. THIS IS THE PRIZE.

The prize is how you do in the long run. The most important thing of all is that, in the long run, you have provided your child with the best possible role model he could ever have. Don't screw it up now by being petty, angry, or sad. Keep your eyes on the prize.

"My Name Is DAD!"

One last vignette. Steve was married for seven years to Mary, and together they had Gabrielle, a beautiful, bright, and engaging little girl. Steve and Mary experienced some "growing pains" in their marriage, and when Gabrielle was four years old they decided on a trial separation. During the separation Mary became increasingly angry at Steve, and he didn't manage his frustration with her very well, either. One Sunday evening, Gabrielle returned from visitation with Steve, and the area around her vagina was red and irritated, an allergic reaction to his cheap laundry detergent.

Mary assumed the worst. And acted on it. Her first call was to her attorney. The second was to the Social Services Child Protective Agency to report Steve for sexual abuse. On the third call she finally got around to calling Gabrielle's pediatrician.

From that point on Mary would insist that Gabrielle call her father "Steve," not Dad. She taught Gabrielle to be fearful of Steve. She was successful, with the help of a bureaucracy that was stacked in her favor, in terminating all contact between Steve and Gabrielle. Steve fought back, insisting on psychotherapy for Gabrielle, and further insisting that he be involved in the counseling. After several aborted attempts, the counseling was begun. After a period of time the therapist was satisfied that Steve presented no threat to Gabrielle, and recommended to the court that visitation be resumed.

The next day Mary moved out of state with Gabrielle, leaving no forwarding address. Steve hired a private investigator to locate Gabrielle, but by the time he found her, Mary had initiated court proceedings in her new state of residence, which assumed jurisdiction for Gabrielle. For the next 11 years Steve fought the system unsuccessfully. But he fought. He made it clear to judges, social workers, counselors, and anybody else who would listen that he was fighting for his daughter. He was not going to let her grow up thinking that he didn't care enough to fight for her. He saw his daughter once in 11 years.

But Steve never gave up. He mailed Gabrielle a card each and every birthday, Christmas, Easter, and any other special occasion he could find. He sent her presents, even though he had no idea what she liked or what she was interested in. He sent her pictures of himself so she would remember what he looked like. Early on, he would receive responses from her that were obviously dictated by Mary, and always addressed to "Steve," which broke his heart. These letters would also contain accusations and statements that he was "bad" and that she was fearful of him.

Worried that Gabrielle would never see these things, he began to copy every letter and card he sent to her. Having no idea about her likes, dislikes, interests, etc., he simply wrote descriptions of things important to him. Poems, descriptions of his family home, accounts of events that they shared when Gabrielle was young, and sometimes pictures of himself and members of his family. Nothing heavy. Just communication. Except that he did request to be thought of as "Dad" instead of "Steve."

When Gabrielle was 15 she was in counseling for issues unrelated to Steve. Steve was aware of the counseling, because he received the bills. She had been in counseling on a couple of occasions before, and he contacted each counselor to offer his support and encouragement. On two occasions Mary abruptly withdrew Gabrielle from counseling when she felt that the counselor might be too receptive to input from Steve. Undeterred, he contacted this present therapist regularly, not protesting his innocence or complaining about how he had been screwed, but simply offering his help and support. His only wish was that the counselor assist in helping Gabrielle to refer to him as "Dad" instead of "Steve."

One Saturday in December when her mom was out, Gabrielle was sneaking around the house, searching all the places where Christmas presents might be hidden. She didn't find any presents, but she did stumble across a weird-looking box way up on a back shelf in the basement. It was full of letters, pictures, and cards for every occasion.

Sunday afternoon Steve was about to leave the house to take his mother Christmas shopping when the phone rang. In a hurry, he momentarily debated whether to answer or simply let the machine take a message. Worried that it might be his mother with a change in plans, he picked up the receiver, and said "Hello."

The small, timid voice on the other end of the line almost whispered . . . . "Dad?"

AFTERWORD: THE BLESSINGS OF FAMILY

Writing this book has highlighted once again the blessings of family. As always, Marion McClure has been most kind, patient, and tolerant, and her smile can light up a room. She overflows with goodness and mercy.

Jessica Ross McClure and Anne Carey McClure provided more education in child psychology than their dad ever received in his years of training. They have been inspirations in so many ways, and they have well illustrated both the joys and pains of fatherhood. After all is said and done, they stand as living proof that joy trumps pain every time.

Although this is a book about fathers, we can't ignore mothers. Bill McClure is the first to acknowledge that he "married up" when he married Jean Carey Mann. A true Southern Lady and mother to three sons, she knew all too well what "little boys are made of" . . . and she didn't even seem to mind. She simply viewed it as part of their charm. May God forever bless her for that.

. . . AND THE USUAL SUSPECTS

Brotherhood Above and Beyond
> William G. McClure, III and Robert Leonard McClure

Best Sister (in-law) a Guy Could Have
> Wyckie McClure

For the Joy of Watching Them Grow
> Kathryn (McClure) Fallen
> Mollie McClure
> Brandon McClure

Friends and In-Laws Par Excellence
> Charlie and Edith Moses and family

Fishing and Spiritual Guidance
"Team Snook"—Bill Rheuban, John Stein, Cap'n Dean Steffan

" 'Dere Are No Voids"
Michael Gordon and Family: Wendy, Alex, Joshua, & Jake

Bad Poker and Good Times
The "Tuesday Evening Probability Seminar"
Ted Shayan, Bill Rheuban, Lon Shackleford,
Ron Heller, Paul Wilkins, Lew Weber, Tom Hegarty

Friendships Over Years and Miles
Pete Keyser, Aaron Ruehle, Ralph Wilson, Jack Morrison,
Peter Oppenheimer, Michael Alexander

In Memoriam
Uncle Bob

MORE BLESSINGS

To my mother, Jessie Saffer, whose fierce independence, forged
through great losses, has been impressive.

To Linda Saffer, wonderful wife and mother. Most of the success of our
marriage and family is attributable to you, for whom I feel such great love.

To my daughters, Amy and Marnie, sources of great pride,
fun, and joy, for whom I feel respect and affection.

To my sons-in-law, Naftali and Shmuel,
men who are becoming fine fathers.

And to Chaim Reuven, Yehuda Chaim, and Yitzchak Dov,
great little men.

... AND MORE SUSPECTS

David and Beth Saffer: who really know how to love and support each
other through good and tough times

Judith Moon: my friend, organizer, and confidant of many years

Asher Elgort, Ron Heller, David Katz, Howard Vidaver, Lew and Jayne
Weber, Bob and Mary Lindsay, Charlie and Betz Gleason,
Vince Guiliani, Ted Shyan, Sharon Beckman-Brindley, and Bob Ciottone,
all respected friends

The gang at The White Castle

In Memoriam: Dr. Mary Vermillion

Finally, a word of appreciation to the senior author of this work,
Dr. Dan McClure, whose idea it was to write this book:
I see Dr. McClure as a deep, sincere, quiet man, who has my respect
as a very talented psychologist, a devoted family man,
and a wonderful friend.

About the Authors

Drs. Dan McClure and Jerry Saffer between them have more than 50 years' experience as clinical child psychologists. Dr. McClure, co-author with Dr. Michael Gordon of *The Down & Dirty Guide to Adult ADD*, earned his doctorate in clinical child psychology from the University of Virginia. He lives near Charlottesville, Virginia, with his wife and two children and works in private practice.

Dr. Saffer, who earned his doctorate in clinical psychology at the Illinois Institute of Technology, recently retired from private practice to pursue religious studies. He lives with his wife in Baltimore, Maryland.

Made in the USA
Middletown, DE
13 January 2015